THE JUST VENGEANCE

THE JUST VENGEANCE

*The Lichfield Festival Play
for 1946*

by

DOROTHY L. SAYERS

WIPF & STOCK · Eugene, Oregon

Wipf and Stock Publishers
199 W 8th Ave, Suite 3
Eugene, OR 97401

The Just Vengeance
By Sayers, Dorothy L.
Copyright©1946 by Sayers, Dorothy L.
ISBN 13: 978-1-61097-024-2
Publication date 8/1/2011
Previously published by Victor Gollancz Ltd, 1946

Dedicated to the Dorothy L. Sayers Society
that has generously sponsored
the production
of this 2011 series edition

For more information about the DLS Society
please turn to the last page of this book

Introduction to the 2011 Series Edition

On the occasion of the republication of some of Dorothy Leigh Sayers' plays, we pay tribute to a most remarkable person: a literary entrepreneur of no mean order, a lay theologian in an age when it was almost unthinkable for a woman to be acknowledged as a theologian, a thinker who pioneered new ways of engaging audiences with central Christian dogmas as rehearsed in the Church's creeds. The final flowering of her work was connected with her rediscovery of Dante's *Divine Comedy*, which stimulated her to produce some of her finest work, including the play she personally thought was her very best. She did not set out to be a writer of 'religious' drama, but her experience of life through a traumatic era of European history, together with her special talents, made such drama part of her legacy to us.

Born in 1893 at the tail-end of the Victorian era, Dorothy was the only child of well-educated parents. She was baptised in Christ Church, Oxford, (Diocesan Cathedral as well as College Chapel) where her father, an ordained clergyman of the Church of England, was Headmaster of the school which educated the boys who sang in the choir. In 1897 her father accepted a Christ Church living in the 'Fens' (drained, hedgeless farmland) about sixteen miles from Cambridge, and together with her mother, a series of governesses and a brief experience of school from age fifteen, she received an excellent education which suited her particular talents. She emerged into adulthood holding to a number of strong convictions, one of which was about the importance of vigorous and clear thinking and speaking about Christian dogma, enlivening the real and varied existences of human beings in all their complexity. Entry to Somerville College, Oxford in 1912 placed DLS among a very favoured few in the Britain of her day, though privilege sheltered no one from the miseries of World War 1 as some of her early published poetry reveals. In any event, her 'Hymn in Contemplation of Sudden Death' (1916)[1] transcends its origins in wartime, though was to come into its own especially in the appalling era of aerial bombing of civilians in the new horrors of World War 11. This is of central importance for the cathedral play written for Lichfield, as we shall see.

So far as World War I is concerned, DLS' detective fiction reflects something of the world of the survivors and the bereaved, and we note here that she never isolated herself from the social and political struggles of her day. Some of her sensitivities are displayed in the development of her portrait of her aristocratic sleuth, Peter Wimsey. He struggles with 'shell-shock' and the memory of having had to give orders which sent so many to their deaths, and as a sleuth he is responsible too for other deaths in a country which still enforced capital punishment. A priority for DLS of course was to find ways of earning her own living, whilst also negotiating a series of love-relationships amongst the somewhat problematic selection of available men of her social class and education post-1918. A man who was not 'marriageable' became the father of her son, her only child, and she simply had to earn money to support Anthony, brought up as he was by a trusted friend before he came to know Dorothy as his birth-mother rather than as his 'adoptive' mother. In 1926 DLS married in a Registry Office a divorced war-veteran, 'Mac', whose children from his first marriage did not live with him.

---

1 In the selection Hone, R.E.(ed) *Poetry of Dorothy L. Sayers,* Dorothy L. Sayers Society, Swavesey, Cambridge, 1996, pp.78-79; and in Loades, A. (ed) *Dorothy L. Sayers. Spiritual Writings,* SPCK, London, 1993, pp.10-11 from her Opus 1.

Life was far from easy, what with the political and economic legacy of World War I to contend with, and the lack of sheer political will to make changes for the general good. Few could view the possibility of yet another major conflict with other than the gravest misgivings. Yet it became imperative to destroy the 'Third Reich' with the consequences for the shape of post-war Europe emerging in the latter part of DLS' lifetime. She contributed vigorously to the thinking about the future which needed to be undertaken to bring about change both for the majority of the British population and for international relationships, not least those with defeated countries. Her detective fiction was by no means a trivial distraction from these important tasks, for in it she expressed some of her most passionately held convictions. For central to Christian faith is unequivocal commitment to truth and justice, without these being identified as specifically Christian in her novels. Thus when on honeymoon with Harriet (*Busman's Honeymoon* (1937) she and Peter together face the fact they cannot pick and choose, that they must have the truth no matter who suffers, and that nothing else matters. This will result in a death sentence for the murderer, and another agonising night for Peter as he waits for the eight a.m. moment of the execution, and who knows what consequences for others involved, however marginally. Human justice and the pursuit of truth will never be simple, and the aftermath unpredictable, hardly free of ambiguity and even of a measure of injustice. As Peter says, 'If there *is* a God or a judgement – what next? What have we done?'

God and judgement were precisely to become the focus of her attention when DLS was caught up into the orbit of Canterbury Cathedral and its Festival of Music and Drama. It was the 'drama' to be associated with the Festival which made it exceptional for its day, given the long-standing suspicion of the pre-Reformation traditions of theatre and liturgy almost wiped out by certain kinds of Protestantism. Canterbury happened to have as its Dean G.K.A. Bell, during the period when its Chapter (governing body) came to think it was time to challenge that suspicion. Having in 1927 founded the Friends of Canterbury Cathedral (an initiative to be followed in many other cathedrals) he found himself with an ally in the person of Margaret Babington, who became the Friends' Steward the following year. Chapter and Friends made possible plays specially commissioned to be performed on the cathedral premises, continuing even after Bell has become Bishop of Chichester in 1929. [2] Bell remains important for understanding DLS' perspective on the cost of the Allied victory in World War II since he became a passionate critic of some aspects of the government's conduct of the war as an Episcopal member of the Upper House of Parliament (the 'Lords').

Both before and after Bell's time as Dean, the plays commissioned for Canterbury Cathedral were by a very distinguished lineage of writers, with T.S. Eliot's *Murder in the Cathedral* (1935) having a most profound impact, given that it was written for the Cathedral in which Thomas a` Becket had been done to death. It also reminded audiences of the possibility of continuing conflict between monarch/government and bishop. Following his own contribution on Thomas Cranmer, it was Charles Williams no less who suggested DLS as writer of a play for Canterbury, a choice not necessarily as surprising as some seem to have thought. She had some experience of stage performance and stagecraft from both school and university and a brief experience of school teaching. She had published a short 'poetic drama' *The Mocking of Christ* in her collection of *Catholic Tales and Christian Songs* (1918); *Busman's Honeymoon* had first seen the light of day as a play for the stage (1936), co-authored with another Somervillian, writer Muriel St Clare Byrne, distinguished historian and writer and lecturer

2. Jasper, R.C.D. *George Bell: Bishop of Chichester,* OUP, London, 1967. See also Pickering, K. *Drama in the Cathedral. The Canterbury Festival Plays 1928-1948* Churchman Publishing, Worthing, 1985.

at the Royal College of Dramatic Art, and one of DLS' valuable friends in the theatrical world. It was a singular challenge in itself to hit on a subject relevant to Canterbury, and this DLS triumphantly did in choosing to write about the rebuilding of the Cathedral Choir after the fire of 1174, chronicled by a monk, Gervase. Thus *The Zeal of Thy House* came into being, first performed between 12-18 June, 1937, in the Cathedral, and on a London stage in March 1938.

In *Zeal*, some of DLS' convictions are made clear, notably in the character of the architect, William of Sens, the embodiment of the principal human sin, pride. The play is also significant for comprehending the significance for DLS of good work of whatever kind, and her grasp of what it means for human persons to acknowledge themselves as creative agents in the image of the divine Trinity. All this most painfully William has to learn. From this point on, some characteristic features of her work in drama began to emerge. Music specially written for her plays was integral to the liveliness of her presentation of Christian dogma, that in turn further heightened in some cases her scenes of debate and argument, testing vitally important judgements about the truth of a situation. Further, her new mode of success as a dramatist was in part the result of her personal humility, willing to take the expert advice of producers and actors as to what would and would not work 'on stage', however admirably written. She was always constructively involved in her productions, in every possible way, making 'cuts' as rehearsals proceeded, whilst frequently restoring her text for publication. Text not used in the original production might or might not be fruitfully used in subsequent ones, depending on context, which might be quite different from its first production.

Such was the success of *Zeal* that DLS was invited to write on Christian dogma for major newspapers, and in addition, received a commission from the then immensely prestigious BBC for a Nativity play (*He That Should Come*) to be broadcast on

11

Christmas Day, 1938. It needs to be recalled that broadcasting was relatively new as a medium for large-scale communication to audiences, and the BBC had high expectations of what it should and should not present to its listeners. Of prime importance for DLS was that she conveyed to her listeners that Christ was born 'into the world', into 'real life', and she had to convey this by sound only. So she re-imagined the world into which Christ was born, engaging not merely with the relevant initial chapters of the first and third gospels (Matthew and Luke) but with centuries of enjoyment of and reflection on the narratives and what had been perceived to be their significance. The main setting is the common courtyard of an inn, in which the characters DLS introduces can grumble about absolutely anything, with differing points of view to be expected from a Pharisee, a merchant and a centurion for example. Joseph plays a central role, and from the world beyond the courtyard the shepherds appear, and it is their gifts which are presented to the child newly born. Finally, we may note that as the published text of her Nativity play makes clear, DLS had not been intimidated by criticism that 'long speeches' would be unintelligible to her audiences, since she went on writing them, whilst allowing for them to be 'cut'. Much would depend on audiences and performers, and she had high expectations of all of them.

So successful was *He That Should Come* 'on air', indeed, that DLS was able to respond to a major challenge, namely, the writing of twelve radio plays (the first broadcast of which began on 21 December, 1941) entitled *The Man Born to be King*. These plays remain unique in their conception and execution, not least in wartime, and her vigorous introduction to the published version expounded her intentions as a writer in respect of 'the life of the God Incarnate' which gives us further insight into her theology. Christ 'on air' had to be credible, and so had the particular human beings with whom he had dealings, right through to the scenes when the risen Christ meets with his disciples, surely a major challenge for any dramatist. There were objections in advance of the broadcasts to listeners being able to hear the 'voice' of Jesus of Nazareth', but the fuss gave the plays excellent publicity, and they have remained a most moving exploration of the Gospels and their significance. Interestingly, given that she had limited the presence of the 'Kings' in *He That Should Come* to the 'Prologue' and the very last minutes of that play, in *The Man born to be King* she seized the opportunity further to explore their significance in the very first play of the twelve, 'Kings in Judea'.

That apart, there is an important thread of connection to notice which links DLS' exploration of the character of William in *Zeal* to the 1941 *The Man Born to be King*. William's principal sin was that of pride; that is also true of Judas according to her brilliant analysis and portrayal of him in *The Man Born to be King*. Between these two productions one further attempt to explore the roots of human sin in pride had presented itself in *The Devil to Pay*, first performed in Canterbury Cathedral 10-17 June, 1939, with a run on a London stage in the next month. (The outbreak of war in the first days of September was to cut short any further production at least for the time being). Writing this play may well have sharpened up DLS' perception of Judas and of Christ's dealings with him. The theme of *The Devil to Pay* is a re-working of the legend of Faustus- hardly easy to handle. In the first place it had no particular connection with Canterbury Cathedral. In the second place it could be very difficult to persuade an audience to take the 'devil' seriously as the personification of evil, for he was likely to be so entertaining as to 'upstage' the other characters, most importantly, that of Faustus with his besetting sin of pride. DLS had the courage to tackle the legend, because she saw in Faustus a figure which we might say was all too familiar in the political culture of her day, though she does not explicitly make the connection. For we can see behind her Faustus not just the 'impulsive reformer' in all his impatience, but the arrogance of the dictator who turns to unbridled violence as well as to fantasy, with incalculable harm as the result. Her attempt to tackle the full scope of Christ's atonement and redemption lay ahead of her, but there was at least one clue as to her confidence in print, for in her 1916 'The Gates of Paradise', DLS had written of the arrival of Judas accompanied by Christ himself at 'Hades gate' (alluding to the ancient tradition of Christ's raid upon those in bondage to Satan)[3]. It is important to bear this in mind to understand the final scene of *Devil*. Here she has Mephistopheles put in charge of the purging of Faustus and the destruction of the evil for which he has been responsible, but with Faustus himself secure in the promise of his Judge that he will never be forsaken, and that he will be met by his Judge/Saviour at the gates of hell. DLS never denies the depths of human wickedness, but hangs on to a trust in 'redemption' on the very eve of war, of a scope and ferocity she and others at this stage could only fear.

In retrospect, it seems extraordinary, given the progress of World War II in its early stages, that anyone should have had the confidence to suppose that there should be serious consideration given to the shape of social and political life after the war, but to that consideration DLS indeed made a contribution. Thus, for example, in her essay in aesthetics and theology, her 1941 *The Mind of the Maker*, a major point is that if human dignity is to be respected, then social, political and economic life must be so ordered as to express human imagination and creativity. This conviction she spelled out in a series of notably pungent essays. Wartime, however, provoked her into writing one play with which she was richly satisfied, and that was to be *The Just Vengeance* of 1946. The maturity of her theological and dramatic vision now flowered in a play entirely original to herself, born of a number of factors. There was the stimulus Charles Williams' gave to her thinking with his 1943 *The Figure*

3. See Loades, *Dorothy L. Sayers. Spiritual Writings*, pp.12-15 from her Opus 1.

of Beatrice (Williams himself sadly dying at the tail-end of the war). The result was her re-reading and translation of the whole of Dante's *Divine Comedy*, sometimes working away at this in air-raid shelters. And at this juncture DLS was presented with yet another opportunity to write for a Cathedral. In 1943 it was far from clear when the war might end, or on what terms, but the Chapter of Lichfield Cathedral had the vision and courage to advance plans for a service of Thanksgiving for the preservation of the Cathedral, and a Pageant to celebrate seven hundred and fifty years since its foundation, which fell in 1945. Given the inevitable austerities of wartime and its aftermath, it is unsurprising that the whole celebration could not take place in the anniversary year. The invitation to DLS to write a play for Lichfield gave her a priceless opportunity to relate Dante's vision to some deeply troubling features of her own era. (In addition to the play, her appropriation of Dante was to speak most powerfully to the reading public in the years after the war, made possible by the inclusion of her work on 'Hell' and 'Purgatory' in the new Penguin Classics series). It was in Canto xxi of 'Purgatory' that she found the phrase which became the title of *The Just Vengeance*, first performed June 15-26, 1946.

The importance of the phrase was to become clear as DLS wrote *The Just Vengeance*. No pacifist, she had come to the conclusion that the war simply had to be endured. That said, she and others had to reckon with a new dimension of war, which was the deliberate targeting of civilian populations from the air. As World War II developed, Bishop Bell for one became a serious critic of the policy which aimed at the systematic destruction of major German cities one by one, in order to bring the war to an end. For DLS there was a personal dimension to the matter of the bombing of civilians, however. She had learned much from Fraülein Fehmer, a music teacher at school, who had returned home to Frankfurt and become an ardent Nazi. DLS' poem 'Target Area' (1940) imagines her former teacher under the airborne onslaught, rightly recognising that in willing the war she willed the means, though their full horror was yet to be discovered. [4]

The issues she had to some extent explored in her detective fiction DLS now confronted in the light of Christian dogma, that is, that the divine court the human judges as well as the accused alike stand before God, that we are none of us free of guilt. Specifically in *The Just Vengeance* she set herself the task of portraying the Christian doctrine of redemption in the light of the conduct of the war. She set the action in a moment of time as an airman is shot down from his bomber, whilst drawing him into the whole company of those who have and continue to inhabit Lichfield. What she wanted above all to convey was what Dante himself had explored in his understanding of 'just vengeance' in the third and final 'Paradise' section of his *Comedy*. This is that 'redemption', if embraced, leads the sanctified to experience the grace, joy and delight of salvation beyond agony and horror. This third section of Dante DLS knew very thoroughly, and drew on it throughout her play, though never completed her own translation and commentary on it before her own death in 1957. Thus *The Just Vengeance* yields irreplaceable insight into how she imagined the significance of 'redemption' for her own time. The popularity of 'Hell' in the immediate post-war period was understandable – the wicked getting their 'come-uppance' as it were; but the challenge of understanding 'redemption' was the greater. She rose to it magnificently, and was justifiably deeply satisfied with the result.

DLS by this time could draw on long-sustained friendships and trust with the professional actors and theatre people who had worked with her pre-war, with all involved surmounting the difficulties of securing and re-working needed materials in very short supply. Music was integral to the effectiveness of the production, and most fortunately she engaged the skills

4. Hone, *Poetry,* pp. 140-145.

in costume and scene design of Norah Lambourne, with her extensive first-hand experience of theatre productions (in the 1950s crucial to the re-staging of the York Mystery Plays). She was also a key player in the production of DLS' final play, for another commemorative occasion. When Mac, DLS' husband died in 1950, Nora Lambourne moved in with DLS, becoming an invaluable collaborator for *The Emperor Constantine* first performed on Monday 2 July, 1951.

If writing a play for somewhere the size of Lichfield Cathedral was a challenge, an even more problematic context was the Colchester cinema in Festival of Britain year (1951) for Colchester's own festival contribution. The connection of Colchester with Constantine was through a legend which claimed that his mother, Helena, was the daughter of its King, Coel, DLS accepted no restrictions on the size of the cast, nor the time needed to perform the whole play (well over three hours), which displays the complexities of Constantine's achievement and exercise of imperial power, including the debate about Christ's relationship to God at the Council of Nicaea in 325 AD, under Constantine's personal aegis. DLS did not spare her audience the inevitable conflicts of the imperial court, leading to the tragedy of Constantine's destruction of his son. Act 3 is the key, performed in London as *Christ's Emperor*. Like William of Sens, Judas, Faust and the bomber pilot, Constantine has most painfully to realise that the cleansing and redemption of his life comes about through Christ, and that is the precisely the consequence of the dogma he had been instrumental in establishing at Nicaea. It is his mother, Helena, who mediates this truth to him. The play may well be said to be of wider significance exhibiting the problems of connecting the dogmas of a church upheld by state authority, with political life and its associated miseries and triumphs. In its London context of St Thomas' Church off Regent Street the shorter version (*Christ's* Emperor) was set for a challenging run, but the death of George VI in its very first

17

week put paid to it. Age-old issues about the human pursuit of truth and justice all too evidently remain.

DLS' work in many genres continued until her unexpected death in 1957. It is thanks to the initiative of Wipf & Stock that we have the texts of these six productions re-published in single volume format, sponsored by the Dorothy L. Sayers Society. Everyone owes an inestimable debt to Dr Barbara Reynolds, engaged life-long with the work of Dante, with DLS' appropriation of Dante, completing the 'Paradise' section of the *Comedy* after DLS' death, editing her letters, writing her biography, and in so many ways stimulating interest in the whole range of work of a most remarkable human being.

The 'religious' plays of DLS, devised for cathedrals, stages and broadcasts were written to be adaptable for performance in many different contexts. They are meant to be exciting, stirring, challenging, memorable, getting everyone involved at the most serious level with issues of inescapable and permanent importance.

Ann Loades
Tayport, Scotland
April 2011

Synopses of the Religious Drama by Dorothy Sayers

THE ZEAL OF THY HOUSE

Dorothy L. Sayers took her inspiration from a monk's account of the fire of 1174, and the subsequent rebuilding of Canterbury Cathedral Quire. She portrays William of Sens, the chosen architect, as eaten away by pride in his splendid work, unable to give glory to God for his achievement. Enacted in the presence of a group of graciously influential Archangels, the play reveals the carelessness of some of the monks, resulting in the terrifying fall that cripples William. His agony brings him to repentance and gratitude before God, and finally to the renunciation of his role, leaving the completion of the re-building to others.

First performed on June 12, 1937; first published by V. Gollancz in June 1937.

HE THAT SHOULD COME

In this first of her plays for religious broadcasting, Dorothy L. Sayers wanted to convince listeners of the truth that Christ was born into our deeply problematic world, in his case, in territory overrun by an army of occupation. Although framed as it were by the voices of the three 'wise men' asking whether the birth of a particular child could possibly fulfil their desires, the focus of the play is on the conflict of opinion (about roads, taxes, and so forth)

19

expressed by those in the courtyard of the inn at Bethlehem. Joseph is given a most significant role, and it is the shepherds whose gifts are presented when the Holy Family is revealed.

First broadcast on December 25, 1938; first published by V. Gollancz in November 1939.

THE DEVIL TO PAY

Dorothy L. Sayers re-worked the legend of Faust as a serious 'comedy', presenting Faust as one who chooses wicked means as an end to an admirable goal: the relief of suffering (while becoming entirely focussed on his own supposed satisfactions). In the last scene, in the Court of Heaven, Azrael, angel of the souls of the dead, claims Faustus' soul, opposing Mephistopheles' claim. With the knowledge of good and evil returned to him, Faustus finally accepts that his evil must be cleansed, with Mephistopheles serving as the agent of that purgation. Faustus accepts his need for cleansing, trusting that the divine Judge/Court President, will indeed in mercy meet him at the very gates of hell, finally redeemed.

First performed on June 10, 1939; first published by V. Gollancz in June 1939.

THE MAN BORN TO BE KING

In twelve plays for broadcasting at monthly intervals, Dorothy L. Sayers drew on material from all four Gospels, keeping the theme of Jesus of Nazareth's divine kingship in focus throughout, while locating him firmly in the social and political context of his time. The first half cover episodes that precede the final journey to Jerusalem and the latter half primarily deal with Passion Week themes. It is on the simplicity and profundity of Jesus' words in the Fourth Gospel especially that Sayers drew on in her own writing for the 'voice' of Jesus 'on air'. The plays gave her an opportunity to explore the many gospel characters surrounding Jesus, not least that of Judas. And beyond the utter sorrow of Jesus' death, the King comes into his own in the garden of resurrection.

The first play was broadcast on December 21, 1941, with the rest at four-weekly intervals thereafter, concluding on October 18, 1942; first published by V. Gollancz in 1943.

THE JUST VENGEANCE

In this play Dorothy L. Sayers addressed the crimes and problems of human life, especially those of the victors in war, in an entirely novel way, by precipitating an airman in the very moment of his death back into the company of citizens of the 'City', in this case, Lichfield. The citizens range from Adam and Eve (Adam himself the inventor of the axe which kills Abel) together with other biblical characters in the history of redemption brought to new life as members of the City, (e.g. Judas is a common informer). Others bear burdens of shame, toil, fear, poverty and ingratitude. Former inhabitants (e.g. George Fox, Dr. Johnson) help the airman to see that no more than they can he shift the burden of his guilt and grief that they all share. There is but one remedy, to join the 'Persona Dei' carrying his cross, finding indeed that he bears their burdens for them. The 'Persona Dei' is finally seen in resurrection and glory.

First performed on June 15, 1946; first published by V. Gollancz in June 1946. Broadcast: March 30, 1947.

THE EMPEROR CONSTANTINE

A brief 'Prologue' by the 'Church' introduces the career of Constantine (from A.D. 305-337) with scenes from the empires of both west and east, concentrating on Constantine's progress to imperial power and inevitably in religious belief. He discovers Christ to be the God who has made him his earthly vice-regent as single Emperor. Summoning the Council of Nicaea at 325, an invigorating debate results in the acceptance of Constantine's formula that Christ is 'of one substance with God'. The implications of the creed of Nicaea are revealed in the last part of the play in which it is his mother, Helena, who brings him to the realisation that he needs redemption by Christ for his political and military life as well as for the domestic tragedy which has resulted in the death of his son.

First performed on July 2, 1951; first published by V. Gollancz in August 1951. A shortened version entitled *Christ's Emperor* was performed at St Thomas' Church, Regent Street in February 1952.

DRAMATIS PERSONÆ

(in order of their appearance)

Actual persons
founder of
Quakers-1600s

THE RECORDER, *Angel of the City.*

GEORGE FOX, *the Quaker.*

THE AIRMAN.

EVE, *Mother of Mankind.*

MARY, *Mother of our Lord.*

ADAM, *the First Man.*

CAIN ⎱ *his sons.*
ABEL ⎰

PERSONA DEI.

GABRIEL, *Angel of the Annunciation.*

CAIAPHAS *(previously an Inquisitor).*

HEROD *(previously a Rich Man).*

PILATE *(previously a Judge).*

JUDAS *(previously an Informer).*

EXECUTIONER *(previously a Roman Soldier).*

AN ANGEL.

A SOLDIER.

PERSONS OF THE CHORUS — *panoramic view of the city of Lichfield*

INFORMER *(afterwards JUDAS).*

INQUISITOR *(afterwards CAIAPHAS).*

RICH MAN *(afterwards HEROD).*

JUDGE *(afterwards PILATE).*

ROMAN SOLDIER *(afterwards EXECUTIONER).*

23

Men	Women
EARLY MARTYR.	PROTESTANT MARTYR.
—SAMUEL JOHNSON.	HUNCHBACK.
LUNATIC.	HARLOT.
POTTERY WORKER.	WIFE.
LABOURER.	WIDOW.
UNEMPLOYED MAN.	MOTHER.
SAILOR.	SLAVEY.
BEGGAR.	PAUPER.
CHIMNEY-SWEEP'S BOY.	CHILD.

Writer (handwritten annotation beside SAMUEL JOHNSON)

✳ *The whole action of the play takes place in the moment of the* AIRMAN'S
death.

24

THE JUST VENGEANCE was originally performed in Lichfield Cathedral on the occasion of its 750th Anniversary Festival, 15–26 June, 1946, with the following cast:

THE RECORDER, Angel of the City	SEYMOUR GREEN
GEORGE FOX, the Quaker	FRANK NAPIER
THE AIRMAN	GORDON DAVIES
EVE, Mother of Mankind	ROWENA ROBINSON
MARY, Mother of Our Lord	DOROTHY BOND
ADAM, the First Man	PERCY CARTWRIGHT
CAIN } his sons {	MICHAEL INGHAM
ABEL } {	PETER BAYLISS
PERSONA DEI	RAF DE LA TORRE
GABRIEL, Angel of the Annunciation ..	BARRY BRIGG
AN ANGEL	DONALD HARPER
A SOLDIER	FREDERICK LAWRENCE

PERSONS OF THE CHORUS

AN INFORMER (afterwards JUDAS) ..	DENNIS RUDDER
AN INQUISITOR (afterwards CAIAPHAS)	JOHN HARRIS
A RICH MAN (afterwards HEROD) ..	CHARLES ROFE
A JUDGE (afterwards PILATE)	PAUL RICE
A ROMAN SOLDIER (afterwards EXECUTIONER) .. .. }	WALTER PULLEN
EARLY MARTYR	HENRY ROBINSON
PROTESTANT MARTYR	JOYCE CRESWELL
SAMUEL JOHNSON	CHAPMAN DAVIES
HUNCHBACK	KAY HUDSON
LUNATIC	LESLIE PARKES
HARLOT	MARY BLACKBURN
POTTERY WORKER	ALBERT HARRISON
WIFE	MARGARET SALT
LABOURER	GEORGE COATON
WIDOW	JESSICA BASSETT
UNEMPLOYED MAN	MALDWYN WORMAN
MOTHER	JANE CARR
SAILOR	MARCUS WHICHELOW
SLAVEY	DOREEN EDGAR
BEGGAR	ALBERT HOUGHTON
PAUPER	BARBARA PRATLEY
CHIMNEY-SWEEP'S BOY	ANDREW SALT
CHILD	MARGARET HODGKINS

Producer: FRANK NAPIER

The music specially composed by
ANTONY HOPKINS

25

INTRODUCTION

THIS play is founded upon two passages, one from *The Divine Comedy* and the other from St. Thomas à Kempis. They are complementary, and together form an almost complete statement of Atonement theology, and of the coinherence of Christ in His mystical body, the Church.

The first, which gives its title to the play, is in the seventh canto of the *Paradiso*, where Beatrice interprets the saying of Justinian:

"My infallible intuition tells me that you are wondering *how the just vengeance justly was avenged*. . . . Because he would not endure, for his own good, the rein set upon his will, the man who was never born (Adam), in condemning himself, condemned all his offspring; wherefore the human race lay sick for many an age in great error, until it pleased the Word of God to descend to earth, where, by the sole act of His eternal love, He took that nature which had gone astray from its Maker, and joined it to Himself in His own person. . . .

"As for the penalty, then, inflicted by the Cross, if it be measured by the nature thus put on, never did any bite so justly; and in like manner, never was any so monstrously unjust if we look to the Person who suffered it, by whom that nature was assumed."

(Para. VII. 19. 899.)

This, with its affirmation of the true God-Manhood, presents the act of Atonement from God's side. The second, affirming the coinherence, presents the response from Man's side: "Whoso will carry the Cross, the Cross shall carry him," and should be taken in conjunction with Rom. viii. 22, "the whole creation groaneth and travaileth in pain together," and Col. i. 24: "Who now rejoice in my sufferings for you and fill up that which remaineth of the afflictions of Christ in my flesh for His body's sake, which is the church."

In form, the drama is a miracle-play of Man's insufficiency and God's redemptive act, set against the background of contemporary crisis. The whole action takes place in the moment of

27

the death of an Airman shot down during the late war. In that moment, his spirit finds itself drawn into the fellowship of his native city of Lichfield; there, being shown in an image the meaning of the Atonement, he accepts the Cross, and passes, in that act of choice, from the image to the reality.

Being concerned as it is with the eternal witness of the Church to the central doctrine of the Incarnation, the play contains no "original thought about . . ." and no "new interpretation of . . ." anything whatever. "Originality" in such matters is out of place: the thought is that of the Church and the interpretation that of her doctors and confessors. Readers will recognise echoes from many other writers, ranging from the Apostles and canonised saints to Charles Williams and T. S. Eliot, and Dantists in particular will take pleasure in picking out and attributing to their rightful owner the lines and images from the *Comedy* which occur at frequent intervals throughout. It is, however, only right that I should make personal apology and acknowledgement to the greatest of Christian poets for having translated and lifted bodily the first six lines of the hymn *Vergine Madre* (*Para.* XXXIII. 1–6).

The curious story of George Fox's vision in the streets of Lichfield is narrated in his *Journal* for 1651.

I should perhaps add a reminder that the verse, as well as the whole architecture, of *The Just Vengeance*, is constructed for performance in a cathedral, rather than for reading in the study, and that the choruses assigned to the Choir were written for music. The circumstances called for a stylised presentation, moving in what may be called large blocks of action rather than in the swift to-and-fro of dialogue; the emphasising of important affirmations by repetitions; and a rhythm enabling the actor's voice to overcome those acoustical difficulties which, in a large ecclesiastical building, no arrangement of microphones can wholly eliminate.

Long lines so you don't lose short lines in the acoustics of the Cathedral.

[*A Flourish. Enter the* RECORDER, *from the* Upper Stage, *with* GEORGE FOX *and the* CHORUS.

Audience part of Chorus.

RECORDER

Verse, not pros.
Rhyme.

You, citizens of Lichfield, here at home,
And you that out of other cities come,
Or towns, or villages both great and small,
To keep with us our glad high festival,
Be welcome to this House of God, which hears
Now the third quarter of a thousand years
Strike on the clock of history. May she stand
To tell her story in this English land
Until the fingers of slow time come round
To their last moment, and the trumpets sound!
Alas! alas! the hardest stones decay,
Man in his rage may blast the walls away— *War*
And make destruction where he once gave glory;
But neither sin nor time can kill that story—
That fact—of man's great need, and God's great pity
Which we show here in terms of our own city,
Playing all parts as best we may. But yet
We, who are actors, bid you not forget
That all these images on which you look
Are but as pictures painted in a book—
No more like that they bid you think upon
Than this small yellow disc is like the sun; *Admitting it isn't realistic*
Though, in a picture, this might stand for that, *Don't be offended*
And the great sun take no offence thereat. —
See now, the citizens, in proper order
Displayed from first to last, with me, Recorder
And Angel of the City, at their head,
Wait here to welcome one who is newly dead.
To him the ageless tale shall all be shown,
And through his eyes you'll see, as through your own.

[GEORGE FOX, *comes forward, having his shoes in his hand and a Bible under his arm.*

29

Fox

Woe to the bloody city of Lichfield! Woe to the bloody city of
Lichfield!

[*He goes about the church.*

Choir (*whispering*)

Lichfield! Lichfield!
Whisper the name of the city through the oblivion;
Let the name stir like the scurry of mice in the wainscot,
In the tapestries, under the floorboards; whisper the name
In the patter of dead leaves on the window; whisper
Among dry bones in the valley of Jehoshaphat;
Lichfield! Lichfield! whisper the name of the city.

Fox

Woe to the bloody city of Lichfield! Woe to the bloody city!

Choir (*a little louder*)

The city! the city! speak the name of the city!
The articulated name in the confusion of syllables;
Speak the coherence, speak the squalors and splendours,
Speak the remembered streets, the familiar houses,
Speak the skyline and the Cathedral spires,
Speak order, speak unity, speak the name of the city.

Fox

Woe to the bloody city of Lichfield! Woe to the bloody city!

Choir (*louder*)

Call the city! call home the blood of the city!
Call the blood out of the alien shadows!
The sorrow with the kindred, the guilt with the derivation,
The flesh and the blood, the bread and the wine of the city.

Fox

Woe to the bloody city of Lichfield!

Choir (*loud*)

Lichfield! Lichfield! cry the name of the city!
Cry in the dark wood and under the iron lintel;
Cry the sweat, cry the blood, cry over the banners!
Cry across the rivers the name of the city of Lichfield!
(*Softly.*) Listen!

[In the sudden pause the feet of the AIRMAN *are heard running from a great distance.* FOX *sits down and begins composedly putting on his shoes.*

CHOIR *(resuming quietly)*
The feet of the young man, the feet of the fallen,
The feet of the forgetful running back to remembrance,
The feet of the future hurrying home to the past
In the sudden cessation of time, the eternity of the city.

ONE VOICE
"For I am a citizen of no mean city."

CHOIR *(loudly)*
Proclaim
Tarsus! Proclaim the citizenship of Rome,
Jerusalem, Athens, Byzantium, London, Lichfield!
Proclaim the Republic! proclaim the Empire! proclaim the name
of the city!

[The AIRMAN *has run up the aisle and stumbles panting on to the steps of the stage.* FOX *helps him up.*

FOX
Friend, thou art welcome. Pray compose thyself:
Thou art within the city.

AIRMAN
In Lichfield?

FOX
Ay,
For thee it is Lichfield.

AIRMAN
The plane took a long time falling;
The fire was everywhere. I hope the others baled out;
I never saw them after I—lost touch.
The trees went past so quickly, catching me up
From behind, and the darkness roared so. The worst of it
Was to have no sense of direction. One comes to rely

31

On navigation. If one knows where one is going
It is not so bad. But those huge vegetable shapes,
And the long processions under meaningless ensigns,
And the noise without speech—it was a kind of terror
I had not experienced; though I was always terrified
On operational flights—but that was different;
One belonged to something; the thing that got me down
Was the sense of belonging nowhere. It went on for ages.
And then, you know, I heard a sound that I recognised;
Somewhere, very far off, a voice said "Lichfield"
Quite clearly; the darkness suddenly focused itself
And was going somewhere, like an enormous tunnel
With the name, like light, at the end of it. So I ran
Towards the name—there was only that to run to—
And found myself at last in my own city.

Fox

Friend, it is very well that thou hadst a concernment
For this or for that; they that are concerned for nothing
Do not come back to this city or any other.

Airman

Well, I am here. What am I supposed to do?
The voice that called me seemed to threaten the city;
I thought about bombing, of course; but the lights are up
And the houses standing—only the people are strange,
As though they were ghosts and could not speak to me;
You are the only person whose voice I can hear—
Was it you that called in the forest?

Fox

                     The word of the Lord
Came to me at the entering in of the city,
Bidding me cry. So I put off my shoes,
For the word of the Lord was like a fire in me,
And I went up and down the streets, crying aloud:
"Woe to the bloody city of Lichfield!"

Airman

                       Yes,
That is what I heard.

32

[handwritten note:] Doesn't find it strange b/c his time is used to hearing about it.

FOX
                As it was given to me
So I cried, and I cried in the market-place
And to and fro in the several parts of it,
And no one laid hands on me. And while I cried
"Woe to the bloody city," I seemed to see
A channel of blood running along the streets,
And the market-place appeared like a pool of blood.
Was that not strange?

                AIRMAN
                Was it so very strange?

                FOX
And all that time, not one of these people here
Stayed me, or asked what I said. They sat unmoved,
Or went about their business, no way astonished;
Was that not strange?

                AIRMAN
                Why should they be astonished?
They have seen and heard too much; blood in the headlines,
Blood in the bodiless voice from the loud-speaker,
Blood in the siren-song and the drone of the bombers,
In eye-witness stories and columns of statistics;
They have hardened their hearts so that they may not break,
Deafened their ears, lest thought should split the brain;
The time has gone by when you could startle people
With words like that—they have grown used to numbering
Death by the million.

                FOX
                Yet every man dies once,
Once, and no more. A universe is extinguished
Every time a soul goes out of it—
The same universe, in a million deaths or one.
The one is the important figure; the rest are ciphers.
The single death which each endures by himself
Is never multiplied, though it is reckoned in millions;
Nor diminished by any division, though a million men
Were summed in a single man dying once for all;
That is the final irreducible integer
Of each man's reckoning. We die into something

33

As we are born into something; but the act of death,
Like the act of being born, is an individual matter,
As thou hast discovered.

AIRMAN

As *I* have discovered?

Fox

Thou.

Fox is using older lang.

AIRMAN

I see. You mean I have had it. Well, I can take it—
(*Uncertainly*) I suppose. What next? Where do we go from here?
Who are you, by the way?

Fox

That which is seen to thee
Is the figure of one who one day came to Lichfield—
George Fox the Quaker.

AIRMAN

Quakers are pacifists.

The Quaker? (*Embarrassed*) I died fighting.
You wouldn't approve of that.

Fox

We are peaceable people.
When a man smote me I turned the other cheek;
He was abashed.

AIRMAN

Was he? it takes more than that
To abash some people.

Fox

We had a most precious meeting,
And many souls were turned to the Lord. I heard
Afterwards, that the fellow who smote me died
In poverty, of an ugly disease. Vengeance
Belongs to the Lord; my hands were guiltless towards him.

AIRMAN

That pleases you? If I hated a man like that——

34

I did not hate him.

AIRMAN

Have it your own way;
But if I were so pleased that something beastly had happened
To a man, because of something he did to me,
I almost think I'd rather feel guilty about it.

CHORUS (*swaying and whispering*)
Guilty, guilty, whisper the guilt of the city.

AIRMAN
I mean, if there is a God—I suppose you know
Whether there is or not—

Fox
Thou shalt know too.

AIRMAN
Why should He do my dirty work for me?
Why should my hands be cleaner than other people's?
I can't explain what I mean, but it doesn't seem fair.
(*Defensively*) I know what you're going to tell me: it was a judg-
    ment;
I don't care; I don't like it.

Fox
I was doing the Lord's work;
When he smote *me*, the blow fell upon Christ
As such blows do; and the judgment overtook him.

AIRMAN
Perhaps he thought he was doing the Lord's work too
The thing's a muddle; that's what you righteous people
Never seem able to see. We try to do right
And someone is hurt—very likely the wrong person;
And if we do wrong, or even if we do nothing,
It comes to the same in the end. We drop a bomb
And condemn a thousand people to sudden death,
The guiltless along with the guilty. Or we refuse

BJV

bomb, and condemn a thousand people
ring death in a concentration camp
ıs if we had set our hands to the warrant.
: have waited for judgment? We did wait,
And innocent people died. *We* are the judgment.
We have no choice between killing and not killing;
We can only choose which set of people to kill—
And even at that, the choice is made for us;
I did not choose; perhaps I ought to have chosen?
I was told to go and I went. I killed; I was killed.
Did any of us deserve it? I don't know.
You can stand there and say your hands are clean;
I cannot. But you were lucky. You could be meek
And go to prison, and not take others with you.
We who are tied in this damnable cat's cradle
Where there is no choice except between bloody alternatives
Have a fraternity which you know nothing about.

CHORUS
Fraternity, fraternity, the fraternity of the City.

AIRMAN (*violently*)
Why did I have to meet *you*? Where are my brothers
Who can lay grimy hand to hand with me
Without dread of contamination? fellow victims
And fellow criminals in the exchange of blood?

CHORUS
Exchange, exchange, in the market-place of the city.

FOX (*mildly*)
Friend, I fear me thou art a man of blood,
And an ignorant man; there is no fraternity
And no exchange, except in the blood of Christ—
But howsoever, thou hast aroused the city.
  [FOX *retires and sits reading his Bible.*

RECORDER
Son of the city, called home by the city,
You have called up the city in the power of exchange.
Look! the city holds out its hands to you.
Whose will you take?

36

CHORUS (*dispersedly*)
Will you take mine? or mine?
The hand of the victim? the hand of the executioner?
The child's hand? the traitor's hand? the rich? the poor? the
                                                            oppressor?
Scavenger? murderer? scholar? tinker? tailor?
Soldier? sailor? apothecary? plough-boy? thief?
How do you understand the bond of the city?
Child of the city, what do you know of the city?

EARLY MARTYR
You that died, did you die in our brotherhood?
I was a martyr for Christ. Diocletian
Was Emperor. There was a slaying of Christians in Lichfield.
Our blood ran down the streets and ways of the city,
And the market-place appeared like a pool of blood.
I know what I died for. Do you know what you died for?

ROMAN
You that killed, did you kill in our brotherhood?
I was a Roman under Diocletian;
They told me, those who would not worship the Emperor
Betrayed the city; they told me to slay and I slew.
I know what I killed for; do you know what you killed for?

PROTESTANT MARTYR
They burnt me at the stake for the blessed Gospel
And the Protestant faith——

INQUISITOR
You died a heretic.

PROTESTANT   One-upping eachother.
How could I tell? I was no learned doctor—
Only a woman, who had learned to love
Our Lord quite simply in His holy Book:
They tangled me in my talk—

INQUISITOR
Away with her!

37

LABOURER

Why grumble, lady? At least you died for *something*—
I never stole the sheep they hanged me for;
D'ye call that justice?

INFORMER .

I was an informer,
Running with the hare and hunting with the hounds—
I stole, and sold my fellow thieves; the law
Needs men like me. Are you for law and order?

JUDGE

There must be order: we must keep the peace—
Sometimes with dirty tools; and if sometimes
The wrong man's framed, or if a stupid jury
Brings in a senseless verdict, can the judge
Do anything but shrug, and wash his hands?
Consider the case of our Lord Jesus Christ—
Judas betrayed Him, Caiaphas accused Him,
Pilate summed up in His favour—the jury hanged Him.
If you are looking for your fellow murderers
You will find more of them in the city streets
Than on the judge's bench.

POTTER

Who murdered me?
I worked here in the potteries, and the work
Poisoned and killed me. All the choice I had
Was, work and die; or, die for lack of bread.
The city is served so.

UNEMPLOYED MAN

I had no work;
If I'd died fighting in the first world-war
A grateful city would have carved my name
Upon a monument—but for the living
The city had no use.

RICH MAN

Why blame the city?
Everything has its price; if flesh and blood
Are cheap, that is the way of things.

38

HARLOT
                    My flesh
Was bought and sold in the market of the city,
Which spat on what it purchased. They who fouled me
Scorned me for being foul, and their sleek wives
Drew back their skirts from me.

WIFE
                    I was a wife,
Hard-working, decent; and my husband said:
"Be still, be modest, do not paint your face.
Leave that to harlots—you're a married woman."
So I obeyed my husband, and he sneered
At his pale wife, and gave himself to harlots.

[*She falls weeping into the* HARLOT's *arms.*

WIDOW (*to* WIFE)
At least you had your husband; death took mine
And left me childless; and I saw the city
One graveyard.

MOTHER (*to* WIDOW)
                    Death was merciful to you;
My children lived to break their mother's heart.

CHILD
I was a child whom no one ever wanted.
I don't know what I did to offend the city
That men should send me crawling through black chimneys
While other little boys were playing ball.
Do *you* know, mister?

HUNCHBACK
                    Look! I was a woman,
And I was ugly. No one gave me children.
Was it my fault that they were never born,
Young man? And what have you to do with me?

PAUPER
Were you a pauper?

39

SAILOR

Did they feed you on weevils?

SLAVEY

Did you sleep in a basement with blackbeetles? Spend your youth
With scuttles and slop-pails?

LUNATIC

Were you a lunatic?
Afraid of the world? of yourself? Were you mad? mad? mad?

[*The* AIRMAN's *nerves give way under this assault, and he retreats
into the arms of* DR. JOHNSON.

JOHNSON

My name was Samuel Johnson; I was learned,
Poor and industrious; and God thought it well
To visit me with a scrofulous disease
And dim my vision. Yet I loved the city,
And was a merry old dog for all my troubles,
Save that a sudden ugly melancholy
Took me at times, and terror of the judgment.
And most of us are so—our learning blind,
Our industry made poor, our souls half-sick,
Our little laughter mixed with fearfulness;
The city is made of such. What did you think?
Sir, what cord was it drew you back to the city?
Fancy or fact? Was it a rope of sand
Or a steel hawser? Why do you seek the city?

AIRMAN

What can I say to you? Sir, there have been times
When there seemed to be a happy and high meaning
In the mere pattern of the city's life; women
Shopping with string-bags, while the ends of the earth
Waited upon them; boys set free from school
Under the drifted gold horse-chestnut leaves
Hunting for conkers; elderly men in pubs
Exchanging slow speech over a pint of ale;
Girls' laughter; the double ebb and flow of the tide
Daily through the factory gates; long lines of streets

40

Silently going somewhere, made for a purpose;
Houses, like safes, with locked-up secrets in them;
The noise of a crowd, mysteriously unanimous,
Like a band, each instrument playing its own tune
To make one music; drays and buses and cars
Moving and stopping for lights or a raised hand;
Pealing of bells; clocks ticking and striking;
Movement of feet and wheels on the surface of things,
Carried triumphant on the hidden intricacy
Of pipes, sewers, cables—the dark functioning
Of distribution. There have been times, I say,
When all this seemed like a miracle and a glory;
And then, like the switching-off of a light—nothing;
Only a crawling of maggots among carrion
In a muddle of petty squalors. If one could find,
Somehow, a way to make the glory endure!
But it only comes by moments. When my plane
Dropped, that was one of the moments. I saw the city
Shine to me. That was the last thing I saw.

Recorder

Son, you have come to the place of the images,
As all men come, whose eyes are not shut fast
Against redemption, drawn to the moment of glory
By that god-bearing image, whatever it was,
That carried the glory for them; some, most happy,
Leaping directly to the unveiled presence
Of Him that is Himself both image and glory;
Some indirectly—this in a woman's eyes,
That in a friend's hand or a poet's voice
Knowing the eternal moment—and you, in the city.
Wherefore you must make your answer now to the city,
And to me, that am the Recorder of the city.

Airman

I'm sorry—I don't quite get you.

Recorder
                              What is your claim
To citizenship?

AIRMAN (*uncertainly*)

I was born here. . . . Oh, do you mean,
What have I done for the place? Not much, I'm afraid;
I was killed too soon. I meant to do lots of things—
Set up in business, marry and settle down,
And start a family; take an active interest
In education and politics; work for improvements
In the economic system; I rather thought
Of writing a book one day; but I had no time,
Except to be killed—and kill. Perhaps that counts
As service? The city should know—that seemed to be
The only thing it wanted of me or anyone.

RECORDER

What matters here is not so much what you did
As why you did it: the choice behind the action;
The deed is the letter; what you believe is the spirit.
Except a man believe rightly he cannot be saved,
Not even by suffering. Can you recite your creed?

[handwritten margin note: What do you believe? Gates of Heaven.]

AIRMAN (*mechanically*)

I believe in God . . .

CHORUS (*picking him up and carrying him along with it*)

. . . the Father Almighty, Maker of Heaven and earth; and in
Jesus Christ . . .

AIRMAN

No! no! no! What made me start off like that?
I reacted automatically to the word "creed"—
My personal creed is something totally different.

RECORDER

What is speaking in you is the voice of the city,
The Church and household of Christ, your people and country
From which you derive. Did you think you were unbegotten?
Unfranchised? With no community and no past?
Out of the darkness of your unconscious memory
The stones of the city are crying out. Go on.

42

AIRMAN (*loudly, and with determination*)

I believe . . .

CHORUS (*overriding him*)

. . . in Jesus Christ His only Son our Lord; who was conceived
by the Holy Ghost, born of the Virgin Mary, suffered under
Pontius Pilate . . .

AIRMAN (*desperately*)

Stop it, I tell you!
That is exactly what I do *not* believe in—
I do not believe in all this suffering—
I do not see the sense of a suffering God—
Why should anyone suffer?

RECORDER (*drily*)
Why indeed?

Go on.

AIRMAN (*angrily*)

We have seen too many people crucified. . . .

CHORUS

. . . crucified, dead, and buried; He descended into Hell. The
third day He rose again from the dead; He ascended into
Heaven; from thence He shall come to judge the quick and
the dead. . . .

AIRMAN

Judgment! wait—there is something I want to believe—
They say there is no such thing as Heaven or Hell,
Or anything after death; I do not know;
It seems I am dead, and therefore there must be something,
Somehow. That being so, I have this to say:
That if there is going to be judgment, I want justice.

RECORDER

You shall have it—more, perhaps, than you bargain for;
Always supposing, when it comes to the point,
You know justice when you see it, or are prepared
To accept it when you know it. Now go on.

43

AIRMAN

I believe .'. .

CHORUS

. . . in the Holy Ghost, the holy Catholic Church, the communion of Saints, the forgiveness of sins, the resurrection of the body and the life everlasting.

AIRMAN

I do not understand a word of all that.

RECORDER

Leave the understanding to the Holy Ghost,
The holy Catholic Church and communion of saints,
So far as they are in you, and you in them.
Now that the city and Church have confessed in you
What they believe, and your memory still believes,
Tell me what it is you think you believe.

AIRMAN

I believe in man, and in the hope of the future,
The steady growth of knowledge and power over things,
The equality of all labouring for the community,
And a just world where everyone will be happy.

RECORDER

Child, that is well; but when you speak of equality,
Happiness, justice—who will be equal and happy?
Who shall have justice done them?

AIRMAN

Everybody.

RECORDER

Do you mean these?

CHORUS

Who will give justice to us?
Where is our happiness? Where is our equality
With the aristocrats of the future, borne on the backs
Of the toiling proletariat of the past?

44

AIRMAN

The past is dead. We must turn our backs on it,
Forget it, bury it. I denounce the past.
The past has turned the world to a living hell.
We must build for the future.

RECORDER

                    You are the dead and the past.

Must *you* be forgotten?

CHORUS

            Must you be forgotten with us?

RECORDER

Must *you* be denounced?

CHORUS

            Denounced with us and the city?

AIRMAN

No! that's not justice! I believed in the future—
I fought and died for the future.

CHORUS

                    Did we not die?
You were our future; did we not die for you? Speak!
What did you do with the future we fought and died for?
Was your world just? Was your world happy?

AIRMAN

                            No;
But what could I do? I had no time; I was killed;
It was not my fault, but the fault of the old people.

CHORUS (*generation after generation, from the most recent to
            the earliest*)

It was not our fault, but the fault of the old people.

AIRMAN

You accuse one another—you try to shift the burden
Back to the beginning, as though you were not responsible,
As though there were something wrong with Man himself,
I will not believe it. The future man shall be good,
Happy and free, walking the world in justice;
Else I have died for nothing. Why was I killed?
I died for your sins—you are my murderers,
Sacrificing me as a victim without choice.
I have no part in you.

CHORUS (*going away*)
        You have no part in us—
No part in the dead, no part in the living city.

AIRMAN

What have I done? I have turned them back to ghosts—
The phantom faces with the unseeing eyes;
I did not mean what I said—oh! do not leave me!
Do not send me back to the dark forest!

RECORDER

You have renounced the past—will you have the future?
Shall we call up the voice of the undead future?

AIRMAN

Call up the future? Yes: I believe in the future,
The happy and grateful future. No; I dare not!
I could not bear it if I were to hear them say:
"It was not our fault, but the fault of the old people."
(*To the* CHORUS) Forgive me, I was wrong: we are victims
    together
Or guilty together; if we have betrayed the future
We will share the blame—and if we have died for the future
Let us believe the future is worth our dying.
But I want to know why we have no choice;
I want to know why there is no justice,
And why it is that everything we do
Turns to a horror we never contemplated;
I want to know what it is all about,
And whether the thing makes sense. I have lived; I have died;
I have a right to know.

46

RECORDER

What says the city
To the son of the city?

JOHNSON

Sir, it appears to us
That this young man is fundamentally sound;
Though sadly ignorant and confused in mind,
Nevertheless, he recognises the city,
And the city him.

EARLY MARTYR

By his and our goodwill;
Wherefore, that he may fully understand
Where, how and why his good will forged his choice,
Sir, we require you in the name of the city,
Show him the Images.

RECORDER

With all my heart;
Let you and you and you and you and you
    (*Indicating the* ROMAN, INQUISITOR, INFORMER, JUDGE *and*
            RICH MAN, *who go off*)
Go play your chosen parts in that great play
Wherein the princes of this world are judged
By Him they judge, and you who are the jury
Stand with the Prisoner in the dock and hear
Your sentence on yourselves; and we will show you
The image of man who was made in the image of God;
And God in the image of man; and the image of justice.

CHOIR

Celebrate man, exalted in the image of man,
Strongest and weakest of things! His life is a span,
A breath—death
Creeps to him through a filter. He measures the stars,
He tames the lion, humbles the unicorn, yokes
The lightning; earth shakes with his strokes.
He makes and mars; plenty is his postillion
And famine fawns at his heels; his wheels
Extend dominion; fear is his running footman.
His sculptured monuments outlast the bones
That built them, and his songs outlast their stones;

47

He heals what first he wounded; he wounds what he heals.
Call upon man in the time of trouble—man
Shall hear. Cry in his ear for fear.
"Save, Lord, we perish!" Cry through the hurricane,
And you shall see and hear
What help there is in the might and the image of man.

[*The Upper Stage opens, disclosing* EVE *and* MARY *with the Tree of Knowledge.* EVE *comes forward;* MARY *remains working at a piece of scarlet cloth.*

EVE

What do you want? You must not disturb Adam.
He is busy inventing something—the old task,
Trying to undo the curse. My sons are out,
Cain in the vineyard, Abel tending the sheep.
I am here alone with one of my young daughters
Whose work it is to weave the purple and scarlet
For the veil of the Temple. What can I do for you?
I am Eve, the Mother of all mankind,
And all my children are very welcome to me.

RECORDER

Ancestral Eve, this latest of your sons,
Newly arrived into the Place of the Images,
Desires to look on the Image of the First Men
Who were made in the Image of God; because it seems
That no man can choose justice, but is bound
Either to suffer or to deal unjustly,
Or both at once, whatever he attempts;
And each one lays the burden of guilt and grief
On the men before him, back to the very beginning
As though Man's very nature were to blame—
And yet he says that he believes in Man.

EVE

O my poor child, you must not believe in us—
It is too true that guilt is bred in you,
Not to be bred out but by being reborn
To a new knowledge by a Heavenly Word,
As we, alas! were terribly reborn
To a new knowledge by the word of the serpent.

48

AIRMAN

What knowledge, Mother? Is not knowledge good?

EVE

Knowledge of good is good; and that we had.

AIRMAN

Knowledge, they say, is power; is that not good?

EVE

Power to know good is good; and that we had.

AIRMAN

How can one know good without knowing evil?
We are not animals, but thinking men;
It is our privilege to know good and evil
And choose the good, or so it seems to me,
And so grow nearer to the image of God.

EVE

O child, O child, that was the serpent's word—
(How well he has learnt his lesson! how the poison
Runs in the blood!) "Ye shall become as gods
Knowing both good and evil." Then the trap
Shut down. We had forgotten we were creatures.
We could not know as God knows, by pure knowledge,
Only as men know, by experience.
What we desired in knowing good and evil
Was simply the experience of evil:
We chose it and we had it.

AIRMAN

All the same,
If there is evil, it is well to know it.

EVE

There was none, till we chose to know it so
What we knew then was what we had always known—
There was nothing else to know; only the world
That God had made and seen to be very good.

But after we had eaten the sad fruit
We knew it by experience differently.
We knew doing and making as labour and sorrow,
Love as possession and lust and jealousy,
Difference as hatred, blessed luck as envy,
The holy and glorious flesh as living carrion,
And death had a new countenance; we knew it
As—death. Hush! hush! we must not speak such words
Nakedly. When we had eaten we knew we were naked,
And made aprons for that and a good many other things.
Death—and birth; it was only after the Fall
That I conceived and brought forth Abel and Cain:
Both of them are my sons—but Cain is the first-born.

CHOIR

Lo, now, the image of the works and ways of Adam!
Knowledge growing as the tree grows in the garden—
Knowledge for Cain, and knowledge also for Abel,
Knowledge for Abel and Cain; but Cain is the first-born.

Lo, now, the riches of the knowledge of Adam!
Riches running as the river runs from the well-spring—
Riches for Cain, and riches also for Abel,
Riches for Abel and Cain; but Cain is the first-born.

Lo, now, the power of the riches of Adam!
Power that gathers as the clouds gather in the mountains—
Power for Cain, and power also for Abel,
Power for Abel and Cain; but Cain is the first-born.

[*Enter* ADAM *carrying an axe.*

ADAM

Cain! Abel! Where are those boys? Mary, my dear,
Run to the fields and fetch your elder brothers;
I have something here to show them. Where's your mother?

[*Exit* MARY *above.*

EVE

Husband!

ADAM

Oh, there you are! Well now, this time
I think you'll say I've really earned my dinner;
Give me a kiss—call me your clever Adam,
Who toils all day to do away with toil
And now and then makes progress. . . . What? What's that?
Company? Why, the more the merrier!
Children, applaud your father's new invention,
Which will go far to circumvent the curse
And usher in the new progressive age
Of leisure and prosperity.

[*Re-enter* MARY *with* CAIN *and* ABEL, *and sits down on the steps with her work.*

Ah, Cain!
Come here, my boy. Here, Abel—look at this,
Is that, or is it not, a useful tool?

 [*He hands the axe to* CAIN.

CAIN (*appreciatively*)

Nice, very nice.

[*He hands it to* ABEL.

EVE

What do you call it, Adam?

ADAM (*irritably*)

What can it matter what the thing is *called*?
How like a woman!

ABEL

Cheer up, Mother dear—
Just call it marvellous.

ADAM (*with offended dignity*)
It is called an axe.

EVE

Why axe?

51

ADAM

Because I choose to call it so.
Of course, you do not ask me what it *does*,
Which is what really matters.

EVE (*meekly*)
What does it do?

ADAM

Increase the power of a man's arm tenfold.
[*He settles down to deliver a lecture.*
You see, the curse laid on the human race
Is labour—without hard, back-breaking labour,
And sweat and toil that leave no time for pleasure
We make no progress. Progress, as you know,
When one gets down to it, is just the task
Of shifting things about from place to place
Quicker and quicker, so as to get more
Of everything at once. (*To* CAIN) If you could reap
And bind and thrash and stack a field of corn
All in one day, instead of many days,
That would be progress. (*To* ABEL) Or if you could go
By some swift engine to your furthest field
And shear your sheep and bring the fleece back here
Within an hour or two, you'd call that progress.
[*Applause.*
The day will come for men to do such things,
By multiplying power in such a way
That one man's hand may do the work of many.
This axe, then, is an instrument of power:
It works upon the principle of the lever.

EVE

What's that?

ADAM

My dear, I'm talking to the boys;
Women don't need to know these things.

EVE

Of course not.

52

ADAM

If you'd not been in such great haste to *know*
There in the garden, we should all be now
Much better off.

EVE

Indeed, that's very true—
My sin was of the intellect.

ADAM

It was.

EVE

So now I must not use my intellect?

ADAM

No; we've been through this argument before;
Women must have no further opportunity—
They can't be trusted. You should have sent for me,
I would have sent the snake about his business,
My sole mistake was listening to *you*.

EVE

Your sin was of the heart. Dear, chivalrous Adam!
You were so noble—never shall I forget.
"If God sends death," you said, "we'll die together;
You are my Eve—my woman, right or wrong."
Kind Adam, I'd not rob you of your heart
Although it made you sin; I hold it here,
And I can twist it round my little finger,
Can't I?

ADAM

You can, my womanly sweet Eve.
Kiss me.

EVE

You won't be angry any more?

ADAM

No, no.

53

Eve

You'll tell me all about the axe?

Adam

Yes, if you like.

Eve

Why, that's my gentle Adam. . . .
(You see, there are more kinds of power than one.)

Abel

I know how this works, Father.

Cain

Give it me,
Abel, I am the first-born. Let me speak.

Abel

By all means, brother.

Cain

Look now, the long shaft
Swung at my arm's length—so—about my shoulder,
Describes a wider circle.

Abel

So the head
Moves faster than the naked blade could do
Held in the hand.

Cain

And that's what gives the power.

Adam

Quite right. When once you've grasped the principle
The formula is simple: Speed is power,
You can apply it in a thousand ways.

Eve (*flatteringly*)

But it needs brains like yours to think it out.

54

CAIN

See here! with this one could cut down a tree
Instead of grubbing it slowly up by the roots,
And shape it to make planks—tables and chairs——

EVE

For me to sit in?

ADAM

You shall sit at ease,
And we will make you things to save your labour—
Things that move very fast, and so breed power,
To turn my hard-worked wife to a fine lady
Living a life of leisure.

EVE

Will the axe
Make me more beautiful, and give me power
The woman's way?

CAIN

A single stroke with this
Would split a bear's skull, strike a tiger dead,
Master all Nature.

ADAM

You shall have fine furs,
Better than those old rabbit-skins.

EVE

O brave axe!

ABEL

Father, if we cut down a lot of trees,
Burned out their centres, wedged them end to end,
Could we not make a water-conduit?

ADAM

Why,
To be sure we could.

55

ABEL

           This morning, Cain and I
Offered our sacrifice and said our prayers
As usual; and afterwards I went,
Singing a hymn, because the day was fine
And I was happy, up to the rocky hill
That bounds my fields to the north—the fields, you know (*to* CAIN)
You would not have, because they were so dry
No crops would grow there. In a rocky cleft
I found—guess what!—a quite new spring of water
Which certainly was not there yesterday.
Isn't that wonderful? It gushed and ran
Among the stones, and some of it was lost—
But if we made a conduit——

CAIN

                What do you say?
You found a water-spring upon your land?

ABEL

Yes. God is good. Perhaps He liked the lamb
I sacrificed. I chose it carefully.
Or else it was sheer bounty.

CAIN

          Sacrifice!
Did I not sacrifice as well as you?
Why should He like your offering more than mine?

ABEL (*gaily*)

I don't know, brother; it was just my luck.

ADAM

Call it God's providence.

CAIN

          It isn't fair!
Why should my brother have more luck than I?
I am the first-born.

56

ABEL

That was *your* luck, brother,
The water-spring is mine.

CAIN

This is not justice—
I sacrificed, I prayed; if God were just
He would reward me too. I am the first-born—
Why should I toil and moil at carrying water
While you, the younger, laze beside your stream
Singing psalms in the sunshine?

EVE

Cain!

ADAM

My son,

Control your tongue!

ABEL

Why are you so unkind?
Indeed you are very welcome to the water.
We'll make a conduit from my fields to yours.

CAIN

I won't have charity, I'll have my rights.
Don't talk of luck or providence to me!
Must I have your permission to draw water?
Must I be grateful? Must I kiss your hand,
That am your equal and your elder? No!
To-day we usher in the great new age
That makes one man's hand as the hand of ten—
I tell you, we'll have no more blundering luck,
But only opportunity and power!
Out of my way!

EVE

Abel!

ADAM

Cain, for God's sake!

CAIN

I'll teach God to make favourites.
[*He strikes* ABEL *down.*

ABEL

Brother!

CAIN

So.

EVE

Abel! . . . He's killed him. . . . Murderer!

ADAM

Justice of God!
Mary, go in—this is no place for girls—
You that are men——
[MARY *runs in, dropping her work.*

EVE

Why are you standing there?
Do you not see that he has killed my son?
Seize him! . . . O Abel!
[*The* CHORUS *make a half-hearted rush at* CAIN, *who keeps them off with the axe.*

CAIN

Back, you fools! I am armed.
[*They drop back.* ADAM *goes up to him.*
What do you want, good man?

ADAM

I am your father;
I charge you by my holy authority,
Put down that weapon.

58

CAIN

Weapon? Now we have come
To the exhortations and the moral sanctions.
I am your son, your first-born; and this weapon—
Is it, or is it not a useful tool?
Useful perhaps for more things than you thought of.
You bid me put it down—by your authority!
By *what* authority, my clever father,
You that put power into the hand of Cain?

CHOIR

Where is salvation? who shall deliver Adam?
Power and knowledge and wealth are only a man's work,
Mighty for good and mighty also for evil;
All men are Abel and Cain; but Cain is the first-born.

[EVE *covers the body of* ABEL *with the scarlet cloth.*

FOX

And the Lord said unto Cain: "Where is Abel thy brother?"

CAIN

And he said: "I know not: Am I my brother's keeper?"

FOX

And He said: "What hast thou done? Thy brother's blood crieth
unto Me from the ground. And now thou art cursed of the earth
and it shall not yield thee her fruit; a fugitive and a vagabond
shalt thou be in the earth."

CAIN

My punishment is greater than I can bear—
Cursed and driven away and dispossessed;
I shall be a fugitive and a vagabond,
And every one that findeth me shall slay me.

59

FOX

And the Lord said unto him: "Therefore whosoever slayeth Cain, vengeance shall be taken on him sevenfold." Thus saith the Lord.

CAIN

Thus saith the Lord—and lets the wolf go free;
I am a marked man; keep your hands off me.

EVE

Alas! alas! must I lose both my sons,
One by injustice and the other by judgment?
O Cain, my first-born, will you not say you are sorry?
Ask pardon? Plead with your dead brother's blood
To speak for you, as the dead lamb's blood speaks
On the altar of sacrifice? What will you do, poor child,
Alone in the desert with the barren earth,
Outlawed by God and man?

CAIN

               Don't trouble, Mother;
Your heart's too soft—I shall live long enough
To breed a race of Cains; and you shall see
The sevenfold vengeance—seven-and-seventyfold—
Before we have finished. Let the earth be barren!
We will build cities, and work in iron and brass,
And you shall bring your corn and oil and wine
And your fat cattle, and your souls, and sell them
To buy that produce. You can keep your axe;
We will make axes for all of you. Let me pass.

[He goes in under the stage. The curtains of the Upper Stage are closed.

CHOIR

God is not served with engines
          He takes no pleasure in horse-power,
Neither delighteth
          in the speed of any man's going;
What though your two hands
          span the dawn and the sunset
When one is the hand of Abel
          and one is the hand of Cain?

RECORDER

So shall the seed of Cain take vengeance on Cain;
Though you slay innocence and outlaw guilt
You cannot undo the brotherhood of the blood.
Every man and every woman of you
Is the whole seed of Adam, not divided
But fearfully joined in the darkness of the double self.
Do you not know it? do you not feel it, all of you,
In the bone's marrow, in the labyrinth of the brain,
In the ambiguity of dreams—the twofold will
Purposing life and death? Do not you all
Suffer with Abel and destroy with Cain,
Each one at once the victim and the avenger
Till Cain is Abel, being condemned for Abel,
And Abel Cain, in the condemning of Cain?

CHORUS

A: Shall we not have our blessing? We are Abel.
B: Shall we not have our birthright? We are Cain.
C: We all are men, and shall we not have justice?
A: Our name is Abel; you have murdered us—
     Are you not Cain and shall we not have justice?
B: Our name is Abel if you take revenge,
     And you are Cain, and shall we not have justice?
A: Cain shall go free, for we will not be Cain;
     We will be innocent though we do no justice.
C: Alas! your innocence has let loose Cain,
     You too are Cain, and shall we not have justice?
A: If you take vengeance on us, we are Abel
     And you are Cain, and shall we not have justice?
B: Brother, what is your name?
C: My name is Cain
     And Abel.
A: Brother, what is your name?
B: My name
     Is Cain and Abel.
C: Brother, what is your name?
A: My name is Cain and Abel.
All: God send justice!
     The blood of Abel cries out from the ground.

61

Fox

Vengeance is mine, saith God; I will repay.

Eve

O no, no, no! that is a fearful saying!
God shall take vengeance? God Himself repay?
Still in man's retribution some small shame,
Remembering the contributory guilt
Which wronged the wronger and excused the wrong—
Some prudent terror of the back-recoil
Of that great clumsy engine men call justice—
Must stay the judge's hand and wring out mercy,
Though grudgingly, and less for mercy's sake
Than policy. But what sort of dreadful thing
Can be the vengeance of the innocent,
Who, being all wronged, need not subtract the score
Of his own debt from the appalling total?
You that cry out so loud for right and justice,
Do you mean *justice*? deed and word and thought
Judged in yourselves by one eternal measure
Of absolute and incorruptible right?
I do not think so. When you call for justice
You would make God your bailiff, to collect
Your legal dues; but not your almoner,
Still less your judge. Alas! you cannot bend
God to your service; yet He may hear prayers—
Sometimes His vengeance is a granted prayer,
When a corrupt heart gains its whole desire
And finds itself in Hell. Children, take heed,
And do not pray for justice: you might get it.

Adam

Wife, I think you have spoken the hardest word
That ever man gave ear to. *Not ask justice!*
That word of yours would overthrow the temples
And bring the state down headlong. Man's first cry
Is still for justice. Children utter it,
Accepting both reward and punishment
So long as they are dealt out equally
To all alike.

EVE

But must we be so childish?
It's in my mind that there is something else—
A kind of mercy that is not unjust,
A not unmerciful justice—if we could see it;
Something that, once seen, would commend itself,
Not to be argued with. The serpent argued,
And all his words were true: but that truth lied.
But God's word was that we should find a Man,
The image of His argument bodily,
Whose heel of flesh should bruise the serpent's brain
Visibly. Will you not pray God send that sight?
For our sad eyes see nothing now but death.

ADAM

Children of men, kneel down and pray with us,
The parents of your Abel and your Cain,
The derivation of your life and death,
Adam and Eve. O God, over our dead
And banished blood we cry. Roll back our sins
That like the leaves of the accursed tree
Shut out the face of Heaven.

[*During the following litany the curtains of the Upper Stage open slowly and disclose the Gates of Heaven.*

CHORUS

Roll back our sins.

ADAM

From the blind skill that has no understanding,
The knowledge that has no wisdom, the glib speech
That has no vision, from the heartless brain
And the brainless heart.

CHORUS

Deliver us, good Lord.

ADAM

From the black chaos that blasphemes creation,
From the disordered will that spews out judgment,
From the dark greed that binds us in subjection
To our desires,

CHORUS

Deliver us, good Lord.

ADAM

From the proud virtues that are our undoing,
From the harsh righteousness whose name is murder,
From the liberality whose name is treason,
From the weak and the strong, from our right and our wrong,
Our worst and best,

CHORUS

Deliver us, good Lord.

ADAM

From all the gods made in the image of man,
From all the worship of man in man's own image,
From the corrupt alike and from the barren
Imagination,

CHORUS

Deliver us, good Lord.

CHOIR

Open the gate! that we have sinned we know—
The sole admission
Brings no remission
Of our despair; life cannot be lived so
In division without vision,
Frustrate, disconsolate,
Knowing so little, destroyed by what we know.
No, no,
Better in a sharp derision
Break, burn, scatter us at a blow,
Blow us away in the blast of the world's fission
Disject, disintegrate—
But yet You hold us to our hard condition
And You will not let go.

64

Open the gate, O Lord, and legislate
Late though it be, for us who wait,
Weighted by our contrition,
Mocked of ambition,
Yet stubborn to believe that You will show,
Though how, we do not know,
Some order in the State.
State terms, state conclusion, state decision,
Speak the name of the City. Open the gate,
Throw open the gate, throw
Open the gate, show
The image of truth in the place of the images, show,
Show!

    [*The Gates of Heaven open, disclosing the* PERSONA DEI, *with*
GABRIEL *and another* ANGEL.

PERSONA

I the image of the Unimaginable
In the place where the Image and the Unimaged are one,
The Act of the Will, the Word of the Thought, the Son
In whom the Father's selfhood is known to Himself,
I being God and with God from the beginning
Speak to Man in the place of the Images.
You that We made for Ourself in Our own image,
Free like Us to experience good by choice,
Not of necessity, laying your will in Ours
For love's sake creaturely, to enjoy your peace,
What did you do? What did you do for Us
By what you did for yourselves in the moment of choice?
O Eve My daughter, and O My dear son Adam,
Whose flesh was fashioned to be My tabernacle,
Try to understand that when you chose your will
Rather than Mine, and when you chose to know evil
In your way and not in Mine, you chose for Me.
It is My will you should know Me as I am—
But how? For you chose to know your good as evil,
Therefore the face of God is evil to you,
And you know My love as terror, My mercy as judgment,
My innocence as a sword; My naked life
Would slay you. How can you ever know Me then?
Yet know you must, since you were made for that;

65

Thus either way you perish. Nay, but the hands
That made you, hold you still; and since you would not
Submit to God, God shall submit to you,
Not of necessity, but free to choose
For your love's sake what you refused to Mine.
God shall be man; that which man chose for man
God shall endure, and what man chose to know
God shall know too—the experience of evil
In the flesh of man; and certainly He shall feel
Terror and judgment and the point of the sword;
And God shall see God's face set like a flint
Against Him; and man shall see the Image of God
In the image of man; and man shall show no mercy.
Truly I will bear your sin and carry your sorrow,
And, if you will, bring you to the tree of life,
Where you may eat, and know your evil as good,
Redeeming that first knowledge. But all this
Still at your choice, and only as you choose,
Save as you choose to let Me choose in you.

Who then will choose to be the chosen of God,
And will to bear Me that I may bear you?

EVE

O my dear Lord, in me the promise stood—
Worst, weakest, yet in me. What must I do?

PERSONA

Woman, that bore the blame from the beginning,
Now in the end bring forth the remedy;
Go, call your daughter Mary, whose unsinning
Heart I have chosen that it may bear Me.

EVE

Mary!

CHORUS

O Mary maiden! Mary of pity!
Speak for us, Mary! Speak for a world in fear!
Mary, mother and maid, send help to the city!
Speak for us, choose for us, Mary!
    [*Enter* MARY, *above.*

MARY
You called? I am here.

CHORUS
All that is true in us, all we were meant to be,
The lost opportunity and the broken unity,
The dead innocence, the rejected obedience,
The forfeited chastity and the frozen charity,
The caged generosity, and the forbidden pity,
Speak in the mouth of Mary, in the name of the city!

PERSONA
In the speed of the Holy Ghost run, Gabriel;
Bear Our message to Mary, daughter of Eve,
That she may lay her will under Our will
Freely, and as she freely gives, receive.
[GABRIEL *comes down.*

CHORUS
Alpha and Omega, beginning and end,
Laid on a single head in the moment of choice!
Pray God now, pray that a woman lend
Her ear to God's, as once to the serpent's voice.

Paradise all to gain and all to lose
In the second race re-run from the old start;
What will the city do now, if a girl refuse
The weight of the glory, the seven swords in the heart?

GABRIEL
Hail, thou that art highly favoured! The Lord is with thee;
Blessed art thou among women.

MARY
What may this be?

GABRIEL
Thou shalt conceive in the power of the Holy Ghost
The most high Child, the Prince of the heavenly host;
This is the word that I am charged to say:
Wilt thou receive that Guest without dismay?

CJV

MARY

Behold in me the handmaid of the Lord;
Be it unto me according to thy word.

PERSONA

Now I put off My crown and majesty
To take the vesture of humility.
   [*The* PERSONA DEI *takes off His imperial vesture and remains in
His alb.*

GABRIEL

Rejoice, O daughter of Jerusalem,
Thy King shall come to thee in Bethlehem.

MARY (*sings*)

My heart is exalting the Lord
                    and my spirit is glad of my Saviour,
Who stoops from the height of His heaven
                    to look on me, maiden-in-meekness,
And all generations shall bless me
                    in the sound of the great salutation,
For He that is highly exalted
                    exalts me, and holy is He.

CHOIR

Who being the Father's Image,
                    the expression and form of the Selfhood,
Thought the equal and infinite glory
                    was nowise a thing to be clung to,
But came to the selfhood of Man,
                    in the image and form of a servant,
Made lower and less than His angels,
                    the Lord of them; holy is He.
   [*The* PERSONA DEI *comes down.*

RECORDER

O widowed city, wake! beneath thy stones
A whispering wind goes stirring the dead bones.

GABRIEL

Rise up, dear city of God, rise up; receive
The second Adam from the second Eve.

RECORDER

Come, thou North wind, and come, thou South wind; blow
On our parched garden; bid the spices flow.

GABRIEL

Replant lost Eden in Gethsemane,
For Love's new fruit hangs from the second Tree.

RECORDER

New age, begin! bring in the golden reign!

GABRIEL

Mercy and truth, long-parted, meet again,
And righteousness and peace kiss one another.

PERSONA

Woman, behold thy Son.

MARY

Behold Thy mother.

CHOIR

O Virgin Mother, daughter of thy Son,
Lowliest and loftiest of created stature,
Fixed goal to which the eternal counsels run;
Thou art that she by whom our human nature
Was so ennobled that it might become
The Creator to create Himself His creature.
   [*During the singing of this hymn,* GABRIEL *returns into Heaven, and
the gates are shut.*

PERSONA

Naked I came out of My mother's womb,
Naked God in a world of armed men.

ADAM

When we had tasted knowledge we knew we were naked.

EVE

We were afraid and hid ourselves, being naked.

FOX

Sheol is naked before Him, and Abaddon hath no covering.

CHORUS

Who shall look on Abaddon unveiled and go down naked to
Sheol.

PERSONA

Mother and daughter, bear Me forth to the world;
Show to them who were made in the image of God
The image of the Image of the Unimaginable
From the place where the Image and the Unimaged are one.

MARY

Good Christian people, you see, this is my Son;
Be tender to Him. It was a very long journey;
The ass was footsore before we came to Bethlehem,
And there was no room in the inn. He was born in a stable,
And I wrapped Him in linen and laid Him in the manger
Between the ox and the ass. The angels sang
And the simple shepherds worshipped; the wise kings
Brought incense and myrrh and gold. Then Herod was angry,
And sent his soldiers to kill the little children—
They died because Herod was afraid of a little child—
But we took the ass and fled away into Egypt,
And presently, when things seemed a little more safe,
Came home to the carpenter's shop at Nazareth,
Where He lived thirty years in silence and obedience.
Consider now the work and word of the Son
Before the ass carries Him up to Jerusalem.

70

The Kingdom of God is come among you. I,
Being the Father's Word and one with Him,
Am here with you in the power of the Holy Ghost.
Thus saith Isaiah: "He hath anointed Me
To speak good tidings to the humble, heal
The broken-hearted, open the blind eyes,
Unloose the captives whom your sins have bound,
And to proclaim God's year of jubilee."
To-day you see all prophecy fulfilled.

RECORDER

The World, the State, the Church shall see it too.
[*Enter* HEROD, PILATE *and* CAIAPHAS *and sit upon the Upper Stage attended by two* SOLDIERS.

PERSONA

Lo! I am come to make all these things new.
[*Enter* JUDAS *and stands watching.*

RECORDER

And some will see and hear and then betray.

PERSONA

Whoso sells Me sells his own soul away.

RECORDER

Behold, against the princes of this world
The banners of the King of kings unfurled!

CHORUS (*dispersedly*)

Is it He that should come? or do we look for another?
Can he do what he says? These things are hard to believe.
I am sad. I am sick—his touch would heal me, perhaps.
He may be a quack. One does not want to look foolish
Or get into trouble. We thought we saw visions of angels.
But visions are dreams, and the thought is betrayed by the wish.

HARLOT

Why do you hesitate? I, who have nothing to lose,
Being so utterly bad, will fall at His feet.
Pity me, sir.

PERSONA

I will. You are forgiven.
Be glad, and sin no more. Sin-burdened souls
Come unto Me, and I will give you rest.
    [*The* CHORUS *draws close to Him.*

CAIAPHAS

What is the meaning of this blasphemous folly?
No man can cleanse from sin but God alone.

PERSONA

Truly. Go now and say what you have heard
And seen.
    [*He lays His hands on* JOHNSON.
        Look up, dim eyes, behold the sun!
    [JOHNSON *falls at His feet. He lays His hand on the* HUNCHBACK
Stand upright, crooked limbs, and walk with God.
    [*The* HUNCHBACK *is healed.*
You that are haunted with a spirit of fear——
    [*He lays hands on the* LUNATIC.

LUNATIC (*shrieking*)

No, no! Let go! Take off your terrible hands,
Strong Son of God—let go!

PERSONA

        Come out of him!
    [*The* LUNATIC *is healed.*

CHORUS

Hosanna, Lord! O Lord, have mercy on us!

JUDAS

It looks as though there might be something in this.
[*He comes down.*
Hosanna!

CHORUS

Hail! Hosanna!

EVE

Alas! alas!
Turn pitying eyes this way, O Son of Man!

PERSONA

Woman, why do you weep?

EVE

See here, see here
This was my son!

PERSONA

Mother, unloose your arms—
Wake, murdered innocence! Rise up from the dead!
[*He raises* ABEL.

CHORUS

Hosanna!

HEROD

What's all that noise?

SOLDIER

A prophet, sir.

HEROD

Prophet? Oh, well! He might start some new craze
To make a dull world seem less wearisome.
Hey, you there! Is there anything I can do
To save me from the boredom of myself?

73

PERSONA

Sell all you have, and give it to the poor,
And come and follow Me.

HEROD

Follow you where?

PERSONA

To the gallows, if need be.

HEROD

Preposterous!
[*He takes no further interest.*]

PERSONA (*sitting with the* CHORUS *about Him*)
Listen, My children. In the olden time
The law was made for sin: an eye for an eye,
A life for a life; requital, not revenge.
But I say this: the Law indeed must stand,
But do not seek the Law. Give, and forgive,
And make no claim; for what the Law concedes
Is your bare merit, grudgingly allowed,
Grudgingly taken; but the gifts of love
Are gifts, beyond desert, beyond desire—
And the meek heart inherits all the earth.

PILATE

You can't do things like that. It is not justice.

PERSONA

Oh, no! there is no justice in the Gospel,
There's only love, which does not seek its own,
But finds its whole delight in giving joy
Unasked.

PILATE

Dreams, dreams. Men are not governed so.

74

PERSONA

Oh, if you want the Law, you shall have law,
Your own harsh measure, pressed down, running over,
Returned into your bosom. What you choose
You choose, and it is yours for ever—*that*
Is the great Law, of which no jot or tittle
Changes. But if you choose Me, you choose Love.

CAIAPHAS

And who are you, to set yourself above
The Law? You know who gave the Law to Moses?
Speak! was it not the God of Abraham?

PERSONA

Your father Abraham longed to see My day—
He saw it and was glad.

CAIAPHAS

                    What do you mean?
Whom would you make yourself?

PERSONA

                         Ere Abraham was
I am.
    [*The* CHORUS *hide their faces.*

CAIAPHAS

    O monstrous!

JUDAS (*hastening across to* CAIAPHAS)
                How much will you give me
If I betray him?

CAIAPHAS

        Thirty pieces of silver.
[JUDAS *signifies agreement and returns.*

AIRMAN

Sir, that your law is good we well believe;
But how to keep it? Will the seed of Cain
Forgive, or seek forgiveness, or be meek?
Was it worth while—forgive my bluntness, sir—
That God should be made man, only to say
To man, "Be perfect," when it can't be done?
A rough-and-ready rule that can be kept
Is something; but impossible demands
Will only serve to make us desperate.

PERSONA

Only Myself can keep My law in you;
Merely to hear My words and nod approval
Is nothing—'tis a house that's built on sand.
I must be closer to you than your marrow,
The sight of your eyes, the thought within your brain.
I say, unless you eat My flesh and blood
And make My substance and My self your own,
You cannot live. I am your bread, your wine;
I give My body to be broken for you
That I, in you, may break and give yourselves
For all the world. No man has greater love
Than he who lays his life down for his friends.

AIRMAN

Is any man worth such a price?
   [JUDAS *goes to* CAIAPHAS.

PERSONA

        My child,
That is a question which love must not ask,
Though some will dip their hands deep in the dish
And sell the love that fed them, Love must bear it.

AIRMAN

Is there no other way?

RECORDER

        Sir, I am sent
To call You.

PERSONA (*rising*)

Angel, is there no other way?

RECORDER

No other way, my Lord.

PERSONA (*to* AIRMAN)

You see, there's none.
It is hard for the flesh to say, "Thy will be done."
[*He goes aside with the* RECORDER.

JUDAS (*returning with* SOLDIERS)

When I embrace him, seize him.

PERSONA

Father, alas!
If this cup must be drunk and may not pass,
I am content.

JUDAS

Hail, Master!

PERSONA

What is this?
Judas, will you betray love with a kiss?
[*The* PERSONA DEI *is taken before* CAIAPHAS, *the* CHORUS *following.*

FOX

And they sought for witness against Him to put Him to death,
and found none. For many bare false witness against Him, but
their witness agreed not together.

CAIAPHAS

Why do we waste our time? Our holy court
Is not concerned with what the prisoner did,
Whether good or bad, but only with his claim:
Now, by the living God, answer to me—
Are you the Christ, the Son of God?

77

PERSONA

I am.

CAIAPHAS

What man of woman born may dare to say so?

PERSONA

I say that you shall see the Son of man
Throned in high Heaven at the right hand of power.

CAIAPHAS

What need of witness? You have heard his blasphemy—
   [*The* CITY *groans.*
He is guilty of death.
   [*The* CITY *groans again.*
                          Take him away to Pilate.

PILATE

What is your accusation against this man?

CAIAPHAS

He has blasphemed; religion has condemned him.

PILATE

In that case, let religion punish him.

CAIAPHAS

The priesthood sheds no blood. We hand him over
To the secular arm. Creeds become policies—
He says he is a king.

PILATE

Are you a king?

PERSONA

Yes, but My kingdom is not of this world.

PILATE

Speak plainly, man; what is your kingdom?

PERSONA

All true men are My people.

PILATE

What is truth?
This is some harmless mad philosopher—
The State cannot concern itself with truth;
Thought must be free; religious toleration
Is Cæsar's motto—we don't care, provided
People will keep the peace and pay their taxes.

CAIAPHAS

This man has stirred rebellion up in Galilee——

PILATE

Galilee?—Not within my jurisdiction.
You should have said he was a Galilean;
Why waste my time? Take him away to Herod—
Passed to you, please, for information and action.

HEROD (*yawning*)

What is all this? Something about religion?
The trouble is, it's all so out of touch
With daily life. Can't you put ginger in it?
A thrill is what we need, but in these days
There's so much competition. What's your line?
The scientific witness? Exploitation
Of fresh techniques? The new psychology?
Old truths in modern dress? Or politics—
God's contribution to the perfect state?
I hope not merely brighter services
And congregational singing. Speak up, man!
Aren't you the prophet born in Bethlehem?
They tell me you work miracles—well, begin!
Show us what you can do. You won't? No thrills—
No sales-talk. Pilate, what's this man accused of?

PILATE

Of stirring up the people.

HEROD

Stirring up? . . .
[*He dissolves into laughter.*
Stirring? . . . don't make me laugh . . . stirring the people **. . .**
Here, take him back—he comes from Bethlehem—
Your bit of boredom and not mine, thank goodness.

PILATE (*waving them off*)

I will chastise him then, and let him go.
Here, fellow, take the prisoner out and flog him,
And that may teach him not to call himself
A king in future.

1ST SOLDIER

Step this way, your majesty.
We'll make a king of you—and crown you too.
[*He takes the* PERSONA DEI *out of sight.*

CAIAPHAS

Pilate, this will not do; the man has theories,
That's always dangerous.

PILATE

Doesn't that depend
On what the theories are?

CAIAPHAS

No, not at all;
You said yourself that truth was not important—
Opinion is.

PILATE

I find no fault in him.

CAIAPHAS

Possibly not; but think what violent factions,
What tyrannous rule, how many bloody wars
Have risen out of words and theories
That seemed quite harmless—even virtuous—
While they were only theories and words.
You would let loose a sword upon the earth
Might sweep your Cæsar from his throne, and split
The Empire.

PILATE

How can any empire stand
Whose laws betray the innocent?

CAIAPHAS

He is guilty;
But were he not, better that he should suffer
Than bring down ruin on the innocent people.

PILATE

The people? . . . Soldier, go to the gaol and fetch
That murdering robber out—for you remind me:
This is the day when we release a prisoner
To please the people. Let the people choose. . . .
Where is the man who calls himself a king?
  [*Re-enter* 1ST SOLDIER *with* PERSONA, *wearing scarlet robe and crown of thorns.*

1ST SOLDIER

Here, sir.

PILATE

And where's the robber?

2ND SOLDIER

Here he is.
  [CAIN *brought from under the stage, in the guise of* BARABBAS.

PILATE (*to the* CHORUS)

Look on the prisoner. (*To* CAIN) What's your name?

CAIN

Barabbas,
"Son of the father" in the Hebrew tongue;
I come, sir, of a very ancient family;
My father has many sons, but I am the first-born.

PILATE

And you—what is your name?

PERSONA

Jesus called Christ,
Son of the Father and the sole-begotten.

PILATE

You know that I am placed here in authority
To set you free or send you to the Cross?

PERSONA

You could have no authority over Me
Except as God appoints you for a judge
To men; therefore the greater sin is his
By whom I was delivered to your judgment.
Yet, as men must accept, I do accept
The verdict of your court.

PILATE

Behold the man!
Consider now, you people of the city,
Which of the twain shall I release to you,
Barabbas here? or Jesus called the Christ?

CHORUS

Barabbas! we're accustomed to Barabbas—
Let us have back our old familiar sin!
Give us Barabbas! we will have Barabbas!

PILATE

What shall I do with Jesus called the Christ?

82

CHORUS

Crucify him!

PILATE

What crime has he committed?

CHORUS

Crucify!

PILATE

Shall I crucify your king?

CHORUS

His kingship makes too great demands on us—
He would be king of body and soul and all,
There would be nothing left of us. Away!
Crucify him!

CAIAPHAS

If you let this man go
You are not Cæsar's friend; there is no room
In one allegiance for both Christ and Cæsar.

CHORUS

Crucify! crucify!

PILATE

This is not justice.

CHORUS

Crucify him!

PILATE

I take you all to witness,
I wash my hands of this. On your head be it.

CHORUS

His blood be upon us and upon our children.

83

ADAM

O sons and daughters, consider what you have done—
How you have pulled the judgment of Cain upon you;
You are all the children of one father—you,
Judas and Caiaphas, Herod, Pilate and Cain—
The sons of Adam who was the son of God.

EVE

See how you have pulled the death of Abel upon you!
Are not all of you born of the same womb?
Now you are all involved in the same disaster,
In the intimate bond of the blood—all you, and Cain,
And Abel and Christ, the sons of Eve and Mary.

CHORUS

Crucify! crucify! let him be crucified!
  [*The voices of the* IMAGES *stop abruptly and leave the* AIRMAN
shouting all by himself.

AIRMAN

Crucify! crucify!
  [*He becomes aware of the silence round him.*
                    What on earth am I doing?
That is not in the least what I meant to say;
I can't think what came over me.

RECORDER

                    The voice of the City,
Speaking in one of its less inspired moments—
Or in one of its moments of greatest inspiration;
For the priesthood of the City is a true priesthood;
And the prophetic heritage still inalienable
By any corruption; the City never speaks truth
So surely as when it does not know what it's saying.

PILATE

The voice of the people has condemned the prisoner;
The voice of the people is the voice of God,
The Empire truckles to the divine voice,
And minor officials do wisely to know their place
And truckle accordingly. Take him to the Cross.

84

HEROD

Take him by all means, so far as I am concerned,
He did not come up to what I expected of him.

CAIAPHAS

This is a very satisfactory ending.
God is avenged, the Laws of the City are safe;
Everybody's weakness has been successfully exploited
In the best interests of society: it is wonderful
To see how all things work together for good.

JUDAS

I have sinned; I have betrayed the innocent blood.

CAIAPHAS

What is that to us?

JUDAS

Nothing at all,
Brother, although you are art and part with me.
There is no exchange in sin; when guilt is shared,
It is only as two men share the same disease
But cannot divide it; each has the whole disease,
And cannot give it away, although he gives it.
In death, you see, none can deliver his brother,
And the brotherhood of Cain is of that kind.
This guilt is yours and mine—altogether yours,
Altogether mine; it cannot be called "ours"—
Sin cannot say that word.

PERSONA

But I can say it,
Because our brotherhood is not in the sin
But in the blood—the fatherhood of God
And the motherhood of the first and the second Eve.
The yours and the mine can belong to both and either
By division or exchange, if you choose to make it so.
Say that the guilt is Mine; give it to Me
And I will take it away to be crucified.
It is all so very much simpler than you think:

Give Me the greedy heart and the little creeping treasons,
Give Me the proud heart and the blind, obstinate eyes (*to*
    CAIAPHAS);
Give me the shallow heart, and the vain lust, and the folly (*to*
    HEROD);
Give me the coward heart and the spiritless refusals (*to* PILATE);
Give me the confused self that you can do nothing with;
I can do something.

JUDAS

You? What can you do?
No one can help me; I do not want to be helped.
Though I cast back guilt and price to the place they came from,
I shall find them again when I go to my own place.
    [*He throws the money back to* CAIAPHAS.

CAIN

There is a place in the desert for them that refuse hope,
Where one may lie for ever and hug the thing that one hates,
And fear becomes desire in the final fixation of choice.

PILATE

I do not think there is any way out of these problems;
One is always at the mercy of events and the world-situation;
One takes the thing as one finds it and makes the best of it:
I do not believe there are any ultimate standards.

CAIN

There is a place in the desert for them that refuse faith,
Where one may fall for ever in a pit that has no bottom,
Endlessly adapted to a fixed monotonous change.

CAIAPHAS (*to* JUDAS)

You will suffer for this insolence (*to* PERSONA) and you, too;
I am not a sinner; I have nothing to reproach myself with;
I have kept the Law and been perfectly right throughout.
Fools and criminals get what is coming to them,
Or how could the City stand? It is quite grotesque
To say that we, who administer the laws of the City,
Are guilty of blood; it is they, not we, who are guilty.

CAIN

There is a place in the desert for them who refuse charity,
Where the iron heart is bound in the bond of its own iron,
Enduring justice, since that is what it thought it inflicted,
Having no humility to see the injustice of justice.

HEROD

I do not see what all this fuss is about:
We are in the world for what we can get out of it.
Plenty of comfort, and entertainment for leisure
Are all I ask for; I ordered no crucifixions;
You earnest people are always crucifying somebody.
I don't interfere—no doubt you do it on principle—
I do not pretend to be intellectual.

CAIN

No;
But there is a place for your sort. There is a place
In the desert for those that have lost the good of the intellect;
Fathomless circles of perfectly meaningless nonsense—
Crucifixions, too, of an unredeeming sort,
In the everlasting exile. This way, brothers;
Here we receive exactly what we have chosen
And can practise on one another to all eternity.
        [*Exeunt* CAIN, HEROD, PILATE, JUDAS *and* CAIAPHAS *under the*
Stage.

RECORDER

Guilt cannot carry guilt; can neither absorb it
Nor yet give it away; there is no subtraction
And no division in the mathematics of sin—
It can only add and multiply guilt with guilt,
Answering cruel injustice with no less cruel
Justice; yet without justice, where is the City?
Only the innocent can ever carry the guilt,
Only the soul that has never consented to sin
And is not concerned to justify itself
Can accept the whole guilt—the open injustice
And the hidden iniquity in the heart of equity—
Carry them away, purge them and sterilise them,
Taking them into itself and making conclusion.
What will you do, citizens, what will you do?

Since you cannot put down injustice without the Law,
And the Law is of sin, and turns to sin in your hands,
Because each one of you is at once Abel and Cain?

Fox

And Aaron shall confess over the scapegoat all the iniquities of
the children of Israel, and all their transgressions in all their
sins. And the goat shall bear upon him all their iniquities into
a land not inhabited, and he shall let go the goat in the wilder-
ness.

Persona

Now am I twice condemned; in the blood of Abel
Unjustly, and justly in the blood of Cain;
All men are so, and God, being made man,
Must walk the road that man chose for himself,
Carrying man's sin and innocence to the cross;
Thus it becomes Us to fulfil all righteousness.

Chorus

Bind on the back of God the sins of the City;
Bind Him for Judas, bind Him for Herod, bind Him
For Caiaphas, Pilate and Cain; bind the wrong,
Bind the wrath and the tyranny, bind the treason,
Bind the fear and the folly, the greed and the grudging,
The disease and the death, the lies told in the market,
The familiar fireside slander, the traffic in blood,
The lazing, the lust, the cruel insatiate wheels,
The needs and neglects, the callousness of the possessors,
The envy of dispossession; bind the City,
The plundered earth, the dull disconsolate streets,
The splitting wood and the sweating stone, the smoke
And the reek, the glare and the glitter, the filth of the kennels,
The slums and the stews, the soil and shame of the City.

Bind on the back of God the laws of the City;
Bind Him for the priest; bind Him for the assessor,
For the upright judge and the incorruptible jury;
Bind Him in fetters, bind Him in just retribution,
Bind Him in discipline; bind the surgeon's knife,
The physic, the fasting; bind the holy war,
The weapons of defence, the armies of occupation;

Bind Him in power and in penalty; bind the rod,
The rule and the righteous judgment; bind the City,
The school, the asylum, the spires of the Cathedral,
The Courts of Justice, the police, the prison, the dock,
The gallows, the stern and salutary institutions,
The state and the standards, the shambles and sewers of the City.

[*The Cross is laid upon the back of the* PERSONA DEI, *and He is led
away about the church by the* SOLDIERS, ADAM, EVE, ABEL *and*
MARY *following, with four* SINGERS.

SINGERS

What is this you have done to Me, O My people?
Was ever such unjust vengeance? Am I not God?

CHOIR

God of the substance of the Father, begotten before the worlds;
God altogether; from everlasting to everlasting.

SINGERS

How shall I answer to Thee, O God my God?
Was ever so just a vengeance? Am I not Man?

CHOIR

Man of the substance of His Mother, born in the world;
Man altogether, in body and mind subsisting.

SINGERS

Is not this well done, that the Godhead should stoop to the
    Manhood,
Lifting it back to God, being God and Man?

CHOIR

Who, although He be God and Man,
Yet He is not two, but one Christ.

[*The* PERSONA DEI *falls.*

MARY

You that are men, made in the image of God,
Will you see all the burden laid upon one Man's shoulder?
For the flesh faints and falls with the heavy weight of the glory,
But the power of the Godhead is enough for all mankind.

RECORDER

Who will carry the cross and share the burden of God
Now, in the moment of choice when the act and the image are
one?
When the angels of Heaven, who are ignorant of sorrow,
Are helpless to do for God what only man can do?
  [*The* CHORUS *run down to carry the Cross.*

MARTYR

I am ready to carry the burden of the oppressor.

HARLOT

I will carry the shame.

LABOURER

I'll give a hand with the toil.

JOHNSON

I'll make a shift to carry my dear Lord's pain.

LUNATIC

And I will carry the fear that shatters the heart and brain.

WIFE

I will carry the bitterness of betrayal.

UNEMPLOYED

I'll take the poverty.

WIDOW

And I the grief.

MOTHER

I will bear man's ingratitude.

CHILD

And I
The ignorance, that suffers and knows not why.

90

Lift up your hearts. Hosanna!

CHOIR

We lift them up unto the Lord. Hosanna!

SINGERS

Whoso will carry the Cross, the Cross shall carry him.

CHOIR

For the whole creation groaneth and travaileth together,
Making up that which is lacking of the sufferings of Christ.

SINGERS

Lift the Cross! Lift the banners! Bring the King to the City!

CHOIR

Meek, riding on an ass, bring Christ into Jerusalem!

AIRMAN (*at the foot of the steps*)

Sir, I understand now what I ought to do.
Am I too late to bring to the wood of Your Cross
Whatever in me is guilty and ought to be crucified?
Whatever, being innocent, is privileged to die in Your Death?

PERSONA

The moment when you meet Me is never too late,
Though the moment of death and moment of choice were one.
Take up the Cross and come and follow Me,
For you shall carry the burden of bewilderment:
We shall find one another in the darkest hour of all.

[*They go up to the place of crucifixion, the* CHORUS *remaining upon the steps.*

EXECUTIONER

It is thought proper, sir, for the executioner
To ask the criminal's pardon; ours, you see,
Is a nasty job whichever way you look at it.
The city needs us, as she needs shambles and sewers;

91

It is our duty to carry out the sentence,
Not try the case; we cannot pretend to know
Whether you are guilty or innocent; either way
The job is nasty; therefore we ask your pardon,
Since, howsoever, our intention is to the City.

[Here the SOLDIERS *crucify the* PERSONA DEI *upon the Upper Stage,*
MARY *and the* AIRMAN *standing at the foot of the* CROSS.

PERSONA

Father, forgive them; they know not what they do.

AIRMAN

Sir, You are privileged to forgive them so;
But we know what we are doing; we, Christ's Church,
Who sin and suffer with the whole creation,
Not without understanding, self-condemned
For our misdeeds, assenting to the judgment
Which we must still endure, assent or no;
Yet somehow trusting that our free assent
Will "turn necessity to glorious gain"
And make our penalty count as sacrifice.
Look now! we are but thieves of righteousness,
Pocketing up Your merits as our own
And from Your treasure paying back to You
The debt we owe You. Lord, will You remember,
When You return to rule us in Your Kingdom,
How ragged, poor, and beggarly we were
Till we laid hands on You, and so accept
What is not ours to give You?

PERSONA

Verily
This day shall you be with Me in Paradise.

AIRMAN

Blessed indeed, thrice blessed are the dead
Who die in Christ. But what will You bequeath
To those who live, still prisoners of the hope
That like a tiny child seems every day

92

Ready to die, it is so frail, which yet
Will not let go its hold on life and us?
Is there some strong and natural tenderness
That can feed hope, and which that hope, grown strong,
Can in its turn sustain until You come
To be reborn in us and in the world?

PERSONA

Woman, behold thy son; behold thy mother.
[*The* AIRMAN *brings* MARY *down to the* CHORUS.

AIRMAN

O Mary of the seven swords of sorrow,
Come home with us, come home; the time is near
When the great night shall cover us all over,
Closer than death and darker, the thick blind
Pressure and stifling darkness of the womb.
[*Here the curtains of the Upper Stage are shut.*
O it is hard, this dying into life,
Helpless and hid, without communication
And with no contact left but through the blood.
Now we are nothing at all—only a pulse
Ticking out time; I am dying, Egypt, dying,
Dying into nothing, dying into nothing, nothing. . . .

PERSONA (*from behind the curtains*)

Eloi, eloi, lama sabachthani!

AIRMAN

I did not know—there is a worse deep still
Under the dark and the silence. Iron teeth
Closing down like a cramp. What is the name
Of the wringing horror? If I knew its name
There is a word of power that might command it,
Here in the bottom of the forgotten world
Where God's face never comes, but only man
Suffers and bleeds in the darkness. You, then, You—
You that are Man here in the dark with me,

93

Tell me the name, that we may break its jaws
And both go free. . . . Oh, no, I have remembered;
Its name is justice; it cannot be commanded,
Only endured. Why then, we will endure it,
Helping each other as we may.

PERSONA

I thirst.

AIRMAN

Once, long ago, You gave us bread and wine
But all my wine has turned to vinegar.
If it will serve, then all I have is Yours—
If there is anything left in me at all
That was not always Yours.

PERSONA

It is accomplished.
Father, into Thy hands I commend My spirit.

AIRMAN — last lines — Consumed
into
Chorus
⇓
reluctantly
joins

This is it. This is what we have always feared—
The moment of surrender, the helpless moment
When there is nothing to do but to let go. . . .
"Into Thy hands"—into another's hand
No matter whose; the enemy's hand, death's hand,
God's. . . . The one moment not to be evaded
Which says, "You must," the moment not of choice
When we must choose to do the thing we must
And will to let our own will go. Let go.
It is no use now clinging to the controls,
Let some one else take over. Take, then, take . . .
There, that is done . . . into Thy hand, O God.

MARY (sings)

See now, you shepherds and mages wise,
How helpless laid in other hands
The very Lord of glory lies
Wrapped head to foot in swathing bands.

94

In swaddling-bands and strong grave-bands.

MARY

Noël, noël, Emmanuel
Is sleeping sound and doth not stir,
Then go your way, before Him lay
Your gold and frankincense and myrrh.

CHOIR

Your funeral spices mixed with myrrh.

FOX (*over music*)

So on the third day, very early in the morning, the women came
to the sepulchre, bringing the spices that they had prepared.
And they found the stone rolled away from the sepulchre.

ANGEL

Whom seek you in the sepulchre, O citizens of Christ?

WOMEN

Jesus Christ of Nazareth, O citizens of Heaven.

ANGEL

He is not here; He is risen as He said; behold the place where
they laid Him.
[*The curtains are opened, to disclose the* PERSONA DEI *standing
before the Cross of glory.*

CHOIR

Speak, speak, speak the name of the city,
The new name, the true name, where the King and the City are
one;
Call us by name, who came
Out of the blind places, to the blinding of the white sun.

95

Answer to our surprise,
Seeing with our eyes,
The obscure demanding
Of bowels and bones and heart, each feeling part
Made suddenly plain in the brain and understanding.
Deal gently with us, because we are so much astonished
To find ourselves thus replenished. Lord, have pity
On our bewilderment; speak! speak peace, O Lord, to the City.

PERSONA

I the Image of the Godhead bodily
In whom the Godhead and the Manhood are one,
Born into time, begotten from everlasting
Of the Father's love, by the gift of the Holy Ghost,
In whom all Heaven subsists; who, being in Heaven,
And being made Man, descending out of Heaven,
Bore for man's sake to set My feet in Hell:
I the end, and I the beginning of all things,
Call My Christendom out of the waste places,
Call the dry bones back from Jehoshaphat,
Call My multitudes in the valley of decision,
Call you home to Myself, in whom your selves
Find their true selfhood and their whole desire.
What has astonished you? Shall not I keep faith
Now with My chosen, and give you all you chose
When you laid your will in Mine in the moment of choice
And bade Me choose for you? When you chose Me
You were made Mine; and I am yours for ever.
That which you gave, you have. All you who choose
To bear with Me the bitter burden of things
In patience, or, being burdened without choice,
Choose only to be patient, whether you give
Your bodies to be burned, your hearts to be broken,
Or only stand and wait in the market-place
For work or bread in a long tediousness,
Think, it is I that stand and suffer with you,
Adding My innocence to redeem your guilt,
And yours with Mine, to ransom all mankind.
This is My courtesy, to make you partners
With God in your own rescue, nor do anything
But by your love and by your will consenting.

96

Come then, and take again your own sweet will
That once was buried in the spicy grave
With Me, and now is risen with Me, more sweet
Than myrrh and cassia; come, receive again
All your desires, but better than your dreams,
All your lost loves, but lovelier than you knew,
All your fond hopes, but higher than your hearts
Could dare to frame them; all your City of God
Built by your faith, but nobler than you planned.
Instead of your justice, you shall have charity;
Instead of your happiness you shall have joy;
Instead of your peace the emulous exchange
Of love; and I will give you the morning star.
Rise up, My mother Mary and come away,
Rise up, My daughter Eve and My sweet son Adam,
Rise up, My city, rise up, My church, My bride!
For the time of your singing is come, and My bright angels
Unwinter hosanna in the perpetual spring;
So enter My Father's house, and there take seizure
Of the crown laid up and the incorruptible treasure,
Where the endless Now is one with the moment's measure,
The truth with the image, the City one with the King.

CHOIR (with trumpet-echo)

God is gone up. . . . God is gone up. . . . God is gone up with a
    merry noise, with a merry noise . . . and our Lord with the
    sound of the trumpet.

[Here the PERSONA DEI goes up into Heaven, with the people going
up lovingly together after Him; and the ANGELS give to each of them
a new robe and a palm of gold.]

CHOIR

Well done, good and faithful servants,
Enter now into the joy of your Lord.

The earth is yours, and the voice of sounding metal,
The gold and the iron and the brass, the clarions of conquest.
You shall command the eagles, you shall laugh at leviathan;
The striped tiger shall sit with velvet feet
At the hearth; you shall be made glad with the grape and the wheat;
Nothing at all shall offend you, no snare shall enmesh—
You shall praise God with the glorious and holy flesh.

The sea is yours and the waters, with the voice
Of the dropping rain; O lute and harp, awake!
Rivers shall not drown love, nor the floods o'erwhelm it;
You shall be poured out with the cataract, ride the tide,
Run with the stream; beauty shall mould and hold you;
You shall fill up the cup of all delight; your art
Shall praise God with the moving and sensitive heart.

The air is yours, the wind that bends the cedars
And breathes in the reeds, the bodiless mighty voice
That comes and goes unseen; you shall be keen
To pierce and pass between a thought and a thought;
Nothing shall stay you or stain; by south and north,
East, west, you shall go forth and turn again—
You shall praise God with the searching and subtle brain.

The fire is yours; the fire mounts up to God
Beyond the angels of the spheres, whose strings
Are tuned too deep and high for mortal ears;
You shall possess that music; you shall go
Secure among the mysteries; the sun
Shall harm you not by day nor the moon by night—
Your soul shall praise God, and your spirit shall fathom the
depth and the height.

MARY (*sings*)

Behold our City, how wide it spreads its gyres,
How great the company of the robes of light!

CHOIR

The City is yours; proclaim the name of the city!
She is set on a rock; she cannot be moved; her foundations
Are everlasting adamant; she stands
Foursquare; her walls are order; her streets meet
In the market-place of exchange; there is joy in her houses;
Her King has called her Zion; she was built without hands.
Proclaim the city!—Hosanna! God is her light.
Proclaim the city!—Hosanna! God is her strength.
Proclaim the city!—Hosanna! God is her confidence.
Proclaim the City! Proclaim Salvation! Proclaim Christ!

THE DOROTHY L. SAYERS SOCIETY

T HE DOROTHY L. SAYERS Society, with now some 500 members worldwide, was founded in her hometown of Witham in 1976. Its aims are educational: to collect and preserve archival material, to act as a centre of advice for scholars and researchers, and to present the name of Dorothy L. Sayers to the public by encouraging publication and performance of her works and by making grants and awards. We have close links with the Marion E. Wade Center at Wheaton College, Illinois, where the majority of her papers are held.

An annual Convention is held with at least half a dozen further meetings not only in UK, but we have also met in USA, Germany, Sweden, France and The Netherlands, studying themes ranging from Incunabula, fungal poisons and Dante, to Education and the Nicene Creed. We have held concerts of music, have sponsored performances of The Zeal of thy House in Canterbury Cathedral, the Bach B Minor Mass in Oxford, and new incidental music for our production of some of The Man Born to be King plays in London. 1993 saw the Centenary of the birth of Dorothy L. Sayers with over 30 events worldwide. Her poem "The Three Kings" was set as a carol, and performed and broadcast in the Midnight service at Canterbury Cathedral.

Our publications include the Poetry of Dorothy L. Sayers, five volumes of The Letters of Dorothy L. Sayers, and, most recently, two hitherto unpublished talks by DLS, Les origines du roman policier, and The Christ of the Creeds. We have extensive archives.

Witham now has a Dorothy L. Sayers Centre in the public library where we hold an annual Sayers Lecture and a statue of DLS with her cat Blitz.

Further information is available from the Society's headquarters at Rose Cottage, Malthouse Lane, Hurstpierpoint, West Sussex BN6 9JY or the web site: http://www.sayers.org.uk

Christopher Dean
DLS Society Chairman
2011